They "Did Everything Right"

"I was very surprised by the attack, I have always felt the campus was a safe place. I reacted instinctively. I wanted to protect myself. I found it's up to the individual in a circumstance like this to decide how to react."

∷   ∷   ∷

In December of 2002, a young woman was returning to her car which was parked in the circle in front of University of Utah's Park administration building when she sensed someone behind her. As she opened the car door, she was attacked by a man who demanded her keys. As the confrontation escalated, she was forced to the floor of the car but staged a vigorous defense, hitting the man, honking the car horn with her foot and screaming. At one juncture, the man threatened to kill her if she did not quit honking the horn.

Two other women heard her cries and after debating momentarily if the situation was real, they ran toward the car. When they arrived on the scene, the attacker exited the car on the driver's side with the comment that "This lady is crazy," trying to pass of the attack as a quarrel. He then walked off. The women immediately notified campus police. The man was arrested and charged with the assault.

All three women were recognized by police and university officials for their bravery with plaques and kudos. The university's police chief said the women involved "are all real heroes," they "did everything right." (see Twila Van Leer, *Deseret News*, January 22, 2003 page B6)

How can you do everything right?

You do not have to be a trained fighter to "do everything right."
You just need to know what the "right things" are.
This book is to teach you those right things
And how to commit to using them for your own

Personal Defense

D1603388

To every innocent young woman who has suffered as a victim
and every young woman who will not have to.

Be Not Afraid

A Young Woman's Guide to Personal Defense

Stacey DeMille Wardwell

Legacy
Book Publishing Inc.

Thank you Trent,
without your encouragement, imagination, and ideas,
this book would never have been written.

Contents

Disclaimer

The material presented in this book is for information, education and entertainment only. By reading further, you accept any and all responsibility for any damage and risk, psychologically and/or physically, to you and/or to someone else that may result from the use of application of any information assimilated from this book. In consideration of reading this book and using its information, you waive all right of damages against Stacey DeMille Wardwell, Blair and Tristan Tolman, Legacy Book Publishing Inc., and all officers, employees, associates, and sub-contractors of the above stated.

Introduction

This is a wonderful yet increasingly violent world we live in. When I was growing up the issues of sexual harassment, carjacking, kidnapping, rape, and murder were not on my mind. My friends and I walked the streets alone day or night and drove around without a care. Believe it or not, hitchhiking was my husband's favorite form of transportation. Were we careless? Yes. Could we have been in danger? Yes. The reality was that these things were happening, but somehow it just wasn't part of my reality. Although these things happened to other people, in my mind "they didn't happen to me."

My children are growing up in a different world. The stories they hear are no longer about someone in a remote far away place; they are about girls and women in their own state, city, and even ward. While my friends and I roamed the streets freely, my children are not allowed to walk to the swimming pool, theater, or even to many of their friends' houses. Although we used to drive around hoping to attract the attention of males in another car, they have learned that they must keep their car doors locked and never give a ride to someone they do not know. My children understand the reality that we live in a dangerous time and I suppose you do too.

If you do not understand that there are dangers, or if you feel like they only happen to other girls, you need to read this book to help you become aware that bad things can happen to good people. With that awareness, you can then prepare yourself with a healthy sense of caution and an understanding of how to avoid those bad things.

Unfortunately, if you do understand that there are dangers, some of you may feel fear—fear that if you were confronted by an assailant you would not know what you should or could do to defend yourself. You also need to read this book to assure yourself that no matter who you are, how old or how strong, you have what it takes to take charge of your own personal defense.

The reality is that you, every one of you, can defend yourself, and you can easily learn how to do it. It doesn't take years of martial arts, it takes an understanding of the enemy, his tactics, and your choices. I believe that personal defense is knowledge and an attitude the Lord wants you to have. He wants you to learn to navigate your way safely through mortality and all of its dangers. He will help you.

There are things you must know about personal defense. The more you know, the more confident you will be in the Lord and in yourself. You will understand the need for caution. You will know that you need not be frightened. In Mark 5:36, the Savior said: ". . . Be not afraid, only believe."

Chapter One

Keys to Personal Defense

"...All things are possible to him that believeth"
(Mark 9:23)

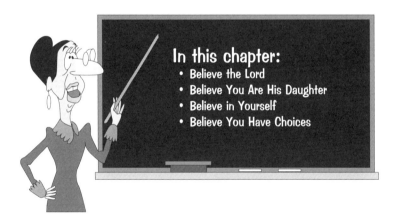

In this chapter:
- Believe the Lord
- Believe You Are His Daughter
- Believe in Yourself
- Believe You Have Choices

Believe the Lord

Remember the field trips that you took in elementary school? No matter where you went with the crowd you were assigned a buddy. Your buddy was there to accompany you during every minute of the trip. Why were you assigned a buddy? Well, if you were stung by a bee, fell in a river, or broke your arm, your buddy would run and get help. If you decided to ditch the activity, your buddy was there to talk you into staying on course. If you simply needed someone to talk to, or someone to listen to your problems, your buddy was there.

If you could have picked your own buddy, you would have picked your best friend, wouldn't you? You would have picked your best friend because you could talk to her and trust her.

The Lord can be your full-time personal buddy. What a gift that is! The Lord is aware of all the dangers you will encounter in this life, and as your buddy, He is there to help you. If you choose, He will be with you always!

Is this possible? How can this happen?

It is possible: The Lord tells us, ". . . and lo, I am with you alway(s) even unto the end of the world" (Matthew 28:20). Do you believe Him? Do you believe the God who created you when He tells you He will be with you always? I do, I know it is true. I know all of His promises are true. He is a God of truth.

How can this happen? When hands were laid upon your head and you were confirmed a member of The Church of Jesus Christ of Latter-day Saints, you were given the gift of the Holy Ghost. (When you *really* want to learn about the Holy Ghost, take some time and look up the scriptures listed in the Topical Guide.) What an incredible gift it is! Knowing that you can't get through this life by yourself, the Lord has given you a gift to help. That gift is the Holy Ghost, and through it, the Lord becomes your own personal buddy to guide you, watch over you, and help you stay on course.

As members of the Church, you have already been given the gift! You already have the Lord as your buddy to protect you in this life if you choose to have the Holy Ghost with you.

Okay, so let's talk just a minute about how you can keep the Holy Ghost with you. Does the word 'Holy' give you a clue? No, it does not mean that you have to sit in the chapel reading your scriptures every day for the rest of your life. But you do have to choose to do or not do certain things to keep the Holy Ghost (the Spirit) with you always.

Here are some examples:

A. Keep the Spirit	B. Drive the Spirit away
Pray	Use bad language
Obey the commandments	Lie
Attend church	Hold a grudge
Read the scriptures	Cheat on test
Listen to uplifting music	Listen to inappropriate music
Give service	Be selfish
Repent	Take advantage of someone

You get the picture. Neither you nor I are perfect (just guessing about you), but if you are trying to keep yourself on the A list, because it has been given as your gift, the Holy Ghost will be your constant companion and thus, the Lord will be your personal buddy. He will be with you always. What greater sense of peace, comfort, and security can you have?

It is important in your personal defense to believe the Lord. Believe His promises: ". . . I will go before your face, I will be on your right hand and on your left, and my Spirit shall be in your hearts, and mine angels round about you, to bear you up" (D&C 84:88). If you believe His promises, you can go through mortality in the "strength of the Lord." You will have His power to help you overcome fear, ". . . for if God be for us who can be against us?" (Romans 8:31)

Believe You Are His Daughter

"We are daughters of our Heavenly Father who loves us and we love Him. . . ." Sound familiar? You have a great knowledge of your ancestry. So many people don't even know who they are, let alone how to navigate through this world. You, on the other hand, know that you are a daughter of God. You know that you lived with Him before coming to earth. You know that you were sent here on a mission and you know that when you leave this world you will return to Him. When it comes to your personal defense, it's very important to know these truths for a couple of reasons:

First: Because you are a daughter of your Heavenly Father, you know that you have a heavenly home. You know that you will return to your heavenly parents and heavenly home when you leave this world.

Every time I go to the airport and see missionaries returning home from their missions, I make the connection between that experience and our experience here on earth. Let me explain:

18 MO. OR 2 YR MISSION	EARTHLY MISSION
Born	Spirit born
Grew up in Kansas	Progressed in pre-existence
Went to Arkansas on mission	Went to earth to fulfill mission
Obedient, served faithfully	Obedient, served faithfully
Sadly depart mission	Sadly depart earth (die)
Family waiting to greet you	Family waiting to greet you
Welcomed at airport with cheers	Welcomed into the spirit world with cheers
Return with honor	Return with honor
Go back to real life	Go back to **real** life
The rest of life ahead	Eternity ahead

When those missionaries come through the door into the baggage claim area, their families are waiting with open arms, signs, balloons and smiles, so excited and happy to welcome their missionary back. The missionary, returning with honor, though sad to leave his mission and the people he has grown to love, happily greets each family member he has missed so much. Searching the crowd, he falls into the arms of his father and/or mother with tears of joy.

I believe death will be much like this airport experience when you return with honor. I can just imagine how excited your loved ones are going to be to welcome you back. Maybe they'll even have big posters and balloons? You will be so happy to be home despite the sadness of leaving earth, which you loved. Then, you will be searching the crowd for your Heavenly Parents into whose arms you will fall with tears of joy.

Death, though it seems a mortal tragedy, is merely a spiritual awakening. If you know that you are a daughter of God and death means returning home, you can be at peace about its eventuality instead of frightened at the prospect. This peace will give you power over fear if you were ever confronted with a life-threatening situation.

It is important in your personal defense to understand death for what it is—a step into eternity. The peace you will gain from this perspective will give you power over your fear of being hurt.

Second: If you want to lay a mortal title on yourself that might even somewhat indicate your status, you could say you are a daughter of a King. Of course, being a daughter of God is much more important, but it's pretty difficult to really comprehend what that means. When you think of yourself as a daughter of a King, it might make it easier for you to internalize. Who would dare offend the King's daughter? Who would dare belittle, degrade or attack her (you) in any way?

You are the Daughter of the King of Kings and the God of Gods.

It is important in your personal defense to believe you are a daughter of God, and that no one has the right to offend, touch, or speak to you in an inappropriate way. Believing in your individual worth as a daughter of God, you will not be afraid to stand up for your honor, your dignity, or your safety.

Believe in Yourself

Believing that you are a daughter of God and thus worthy of defending, you now need to believe that you have the power within you to defend yourself. You really do. As a daughter of God, you are created in His image (well, technically in our Heavenly Mother's image)—you have a divine nature which means you have godly attributes. The Lord expects you to live up to your divine potential. I believe each of you have the attributes necessary to succeed in your own personal defense.

> ☾ You need to accept the fact that from this moment on, your situation and your future is in capable hands—yours. ☽
>
> -Unknown

When I speak of personal defense, I mean everything that is personal to you, every part of you. This means defending not only your body, but also your spirit. You have the right to determine what is offensive to you and put a stop to it.

QUIZ: What Do You Do?

You are getting a drink at the drinking fountain. A boy comes behind you and touches you inappropriately on your bent-over lower half. (I don't like to be crude, but if you haven't figured out where I'm going with this—it's your buttocks!) OR You are leaning against a wall waiting for a classroom to open, and a boy squeezes past you, very obviously rubbing against your chest OR You are waiting in line at an amusement park and some guy begins making suggestive or crude comments about your body.

Choices:

      ❑ Ignore him

A) ❑ Ask him to stop

      ❑ Try to avoid him

          OR

      ❑ Look him squarely in the eyes and say "Get away from me!"

B) ❑ Elbow him in the stomach, look him squarely in the eyes and tell him to stop it!

These behaviors are offensive to you, your body, and your spirit. I know similar things happen in hallways, lines, crowds, parties, and dances everywhere. These kinds of boys are predators just like the ones you'll be learning about later in this book. Predators come in many different packages, from those out to demean you for a "power rush" to those with violent intentions. I have just described some of the more common ones you will run into. These predators get their kicks or their "power surge" from attacking your honor and self-respect. They prey on anyone who will let them. They are called bullies and they are looking for an easy target.

Answers:

A) If you choose any of the A answers, you will continue to be this guy's victim. He has found an easy target, someone who won't stand up for herself.

B) If you choose any of the B answers, you will no longer be his victim. He will move on to find an easier target. And it was **you** who stopped it.

It is important in your personal defense to believe in yourself. You must believe that you are worthy of defending and that you have the power to do it!! Believing in your divine nature will help you overcome your fear of inadequacy and give you power to initiate your own personal defense if necessary.

Believe You Have Choices

"Choice" will be the theme of the rest of this book. As we talk about personal defense, my greatest desire is for you to realize that you have choices! Often when you hear assault stories about a girl being taken, raped, or murdered, you feel helpless. You wonder what you would have done or could have done if you were the one under attack. You get scared. This is what you must know: You will always have choices up to a point!

> It's choice—
> not chance—
> that determines
> your destiny.
>
> -Jean Nidetch

Whether it's to lock your car doors, confront a boy who is demeaning you, take a friend along as you're traveling, avoid certain parties, or fend off a physical attack, you will make choices every day which can affect your safety. When it comes to your personal defense, it's important to understand your best choices and then practice making them.

This book is to help you understand what those choices are. As you read the following chapters, you will see the word CHOICE? in the middle of stories and examples. This is to remind you that as threatening as a situation is, you have a choice at that point. Your choice will be to submit or resist. As you

continue through the story and see the conclusion, notice how the choice determines the outcome.

RESIST: You do not go along with your attacker, instead you stand up to him; yell, run, or fight, anything that would interrupt his planned assault on you.

It is important in your personal defense to believe you have

SUBMIT: You go along with your attacker and do what he tells you.

choices. Believing you have choices will help you overcome

your fear of helplessness and give you the confidence to can handle any situation you may be faced with.

Remember:
It is important in your personal defense to believe:
- The Lord and His promises.
- Death is a step into eternity.
- As a daughter of God, no one has the right to offend, touch, or speak to you in an inappropriate way.
- You are worthy of defending and you have the power to defend yourself.
- You have choices.

Chapter Two

Choose What You Will and Will Not Defend

"Never kick a fresh turd on a hot day."
—Harry S. Truman

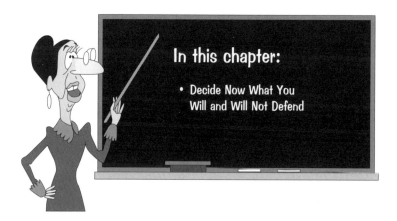

In this chapter:

- Decide Now What You Will and Will Not Defend

Decide Now What You Will and Will Not Defend

Have you ever heard, "There's no time like the present?" The statement suggests that if there is something you can do right now—there won't be a better time, so you should just do it! When it comes to deciding what you will and will not defend—now is the time you should do it.

Making a split second decision on the spot about whether you will defend your purse, car, dignity, or life is not a great idea. Your ability to think rationally under extreme pressure will be seriously impaired. This is a decision you need to make ahead of time, while you can think clearly, not when you're in an adrenaline-charged situation. Remember the Boy Scout motto: "Be Prepared"? It's now your motto for personal defense too! Make your decisions now (well actually, why don't you wait until you finish reading this book) and prepare yourself for the "what if's." If your decisions are already made, you will be prepared to react rationally, the way you truly want to, if the situation ever does happen.

To help you make that decision, let me give you a sobering fact: anytime there is a physical confrontation, someone is likely to get hurt and that someone is very likely to be you. That's it, that's just the way it is. Taking a defensive position that leads to violence simply for your purse, or even your car, is unwise. There is too much at risk—you— your life! Why risk injury or death either to yourself or to your assailant for something that can be replaced?

It Could Happen

You are walking from your car to go to a movie and a man demands your purse. CHOICE? Give it to him. If he tries to intimidate you into his car, to a more secluded area, or gives any indication that he is not done with you yet, CHOICE? immediately defend yourself. Now he is messing with you, not just your stuff.

 Stuff is just stuff and you can replace it. You don't need to prove anything to anyone. Who "wins" the purse is of little importance. When we're talking about losing property, it is not a pride issue. This is an issue of your best chance of survival with the least amount of injury to yourself or your assailant. If an assailant demanded my purse, the fact that I am a second-degree Black-Belt in Tae Kwon Do and have been practicing and teaching personal

defense for the last 10 years makes no difference. If it's stuff they want, then it's stuff they'll get. My life is just not worth the risk and neither is yours.

However, if for one second you feel that your life or virtue is threatened in any way, it's time to transform and put up a RAGING defense (more about that in chapter 7). You are a daughter of God, unique and wonderful. No one has the right to touch you or hurt you in any way. Did I say no one? I really mean no one has the right to offend you emotionally or physically. NO ONE!

> ☾ Make certain decisions only once. . . . We can make a single decision about certain things that we will incorporate in our lives and then make them ours. . . .☽
> –Pres. Spencer W. Kimball

Remember:
- Decide now what you will and will not defend.
- Your property is not worth a physical confrontation.
- Your life and self-respect are worth defending.

Chapter Three

Choose to Learn about Assaults & Assailants

"You can observe a lot by watching."
—Yogi Berra

In this chapter:
- What Is an Assault?
- Who Are Assailants?
- Assault Has a Pattern
- Your Psychological Advantage

What Is an Assault?

> **ASSAULT** is a fancy word for a violent verbal, sexual, or physical attack.

Assault is a general term that includes many aggressive behaviors. The general categories are:

TYPE OF ASSAULT	RESULT
Simple assault	no weapon, less-than-serious bodily injury intended
Aggravated assault	weapon used, serious bodily injury intended
Sexual assault	sexual violence against victim intended
Take-advantage assault	injury to your spirit, self esteem, and sometimes finances intended

The take-advantage assault is my own term. I use this to describe the many ways in which non-violent predators can still injure you. Though your life may not be in danger, they leave their marks on you emotionally and sometimes financially.

Who Are Assailants?

Anyone who would take advantage of you emotionally, financially, or physically is an assailant. Don't assume a predator

ASSAILANT is a fancy word for predator, perpetrator, and low-life, AKA the jerk that assaulted you

will tip you off by the way he looks. Assailants can be male or female, large or small, any nationality or race. I will use "he" because it is our common conception of a predator, though it could easily be a she. The only thing all assailants have in common is that they are all

It Happened

I was at a gas station with my 14-year-old daughter. Across from us at another pump was a pretty beat-up car with some rough-looking guys in it. As soon as I stepped out of the car to pump the gas, my daughter locked the doors. (Thanks a lot, leave me out there with them!)

My point with this story is that because the people in the car across from us looked scary, my daughter was on her guard.

predators. Like an animal hunting prey in the wild, a human predator is hunting for his victim.

Assailants come in all sizes, shapes, and genders. We tend to think of an assailant as a big, scary-looking man, someone who would stand out in a crowd and might as well have a sign with "mean guy" stamped across his forehead. Actually, it would be nice if assailants would identify themselves this way.

Unfortunately, because they are trying to commit acts in secret, they generally try to blend in with the scenery—like the man who dressed as a doctor and roamed the halls of a hospital, found a woman alone, and raped and murdered her. Because he "looked" like every other doctor, he blended in and was allowed to walk the hospital freely, even though the rest of the staff didn't know him.

Assailants may pose as painters, florists, ministers, exterminators, workmen, and even policemen. You name it, if it fits into the scenery, it's been used. They may be walking their dog or jogging in your neighborhood. They could show up at your door posing as absolutely anything. It could be a husband/wife team—they could even have a baby.

Your guard should always be up. Many people are lulled into complacency because they don't see anything suspicious. They do something they wouldn't normally do such as:

- Let someone into their home.
- Walk to their car with them.
- Give them their name and address.
- Let them help with their groceries.
- Offer a ride to someone who looks "nice."

 If you wouldn't do something for a "scary-looking" person, you shouldn't do it for a "nice-looking" person either!

That doesn't mean that "scary-looking" people are off the hook, it really means that no one is off the hook. You can't trust your eyes; you need to use common sense and trust your feelings (more about that in chapter 6).

 You should always be on your guard.
You should always lock your doors (car, house, office, etc.).
A predator usually doesn't look any different than your next-door neighbor.
Most predators actually try to blend in.

Assault Has A Pattern

Though there is nothing consistent with the way an assailant looks, there is usually a pattern to his assault. Do you remember finding patterns in grade school? Your teacher would give you a row of shapes or numbers that repeated themselves over and over. When the exercise stopped, you were to figure out which shape or number came next. Knowing how the pattern was laid out, you were able to recognize the shape or number that would allow the pattern to continue.

Fortunately, there is also a pattern to an assault. Certain behaviors will repeat themselves over and over. (The reason these behaviors are repeated over and over is because they tend to be very successful for assailants.) However, if you know what those behaviors are, you can recognize when that pattern is repeating itself on you and, predicting what will come next, you can interrupt the pattern. In this way, you can stop an assault in the early stages before it ever gets to the part of the pattern in which an attack occurs.

ASSAULT PATTERN	YOUR DEFENSES
Target	Alert
Test	Avoid
Attack	Action

Your Psychological Advantage

Dr. Judith Fein, Ph.D., a nationally recognized self-defense expert, has stated, "I fully believe that self-defense is at least seventy-five percent psychological."[1] The greatest asset you have in your personal defense is to know your enemy, his game plan, and how to interrupt it. This knowledge, if applied (meaning you *use* it), will dramatically decrease the chance that you will ever be physically attacked.

That may sound like a pretty bold statement but it is a fact. As Dr. Fein suggests, most of the time, by practicing the personal defense "attitudes" you will find in the next few chapters, you will be able to stop an assault in the "target or test" stage before it ever escalates into a physical attack. The more you know, the bigger psychological advantage you will have and the less likely you will be to let an assault play out on you without recognizing and stopping it.

Now that you know there is a pattern to an assault, let's look at that pattern and learn how to interrupt it.

Remember:

- There are many types of assaults.
- Assailants come in all sizes, shapes, gender and race.
- Don't be lured into anything just because someone looks "nice."
- Knowing the Assault Pattern will help you interrupt it in the early stages before it leads to a physical attack.

---

[1] Judith Fein, Ph.D., *How to Fight Back and Win, The Joy of Self-Defense*, Sebastopol, California: Torrance Publishing Company, p. 22.

Chapter Four

Choose Not to Be a Target

"Confidence is a habit that can be developed by acting as if you already had the confidence you desire to have."
—Brian Tracy

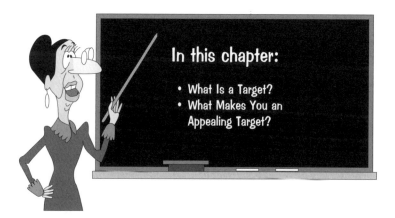

In this chapter:

- What Is a Target?
- What Makes You an Appealing Target?

What Is a Target?

The first step in the assault pattern is "target." In any assault, the assailant must first find a victim. Just as we zero in on a target at a rifle range, a predator is focused on finding just the right person to zero in on. He's looking for a bulls-eye, someone that he will "target" as his next victim.

Choose not to be a target! You might be saying: "Of course I choose not to be a target, who'd want to be one of those?" Saying that you can choose almost sounds too simple, doesn't it? But you actually do have a say in the matter by making choices that will prevent you from being an appealing target. You can help yourself choose not to be a target by being alert.

 Be alert to your surroundings: "Being alert to your surroundings is enough to prevent 95 percent of all attacks."[1] Being alert is one of the most important tips you can use in your personal defense. Being alert to your surroundings suggests being watchful, careful, and aware of possible problems and dangers everywhere you go.

 Be alert to what makes you an appealing target.

What Makes You an Appealing Target?

First, being female: Women are perceived as weaker than men. There is nothing you can do about the fact that being female makes you a prime target.

ALERT What you can do is be smart about how you present yourself. Do not call attention to yourself. Tight, skimpy, or expensive clothes, flashy jewelry, and flaunting money may entice a predator to look your way more closely. Remember, predators not only come in every size and gender, they come with varied agendas too. Some are out to harass and embarrass, some are out for your money, and some are out with even more sinister intentions. To protect yourself from any, you must be alert to all.

---

[1] Richard J. Machowicz in Dana Hudepohl, "15 Ways to Save Your Life," *Glamour*, August 2000, p.120.

It Happened

Mindy was traveling with her family on the MARTA system in downtown Atlanta at Christmas time. There were few people on the train and the family was relaxed and enjoying the ride. CHOICE? She decided to take this opportunity to clean out her purse. She pulled out everything including her wallet which she opened to count her money. About the time the family got off the train and walked to Underground Atlanta to do some shopping, Mindy realized that her wallet and the $600 in it was gone. After an intense search involving the police, Mindy realized that the only place someone could have taken her wallet was on that Metro train. It was amazing to her and her family how invisible the thief had been.

ALERT

Don't flash cash or anything else you want to keep hold of.

SAFETY TIP:

A friend of mine who worked for the State Penitentiary was told to dress very conservatively with loose-fitting clothing so she would not draw attention to herself while at work. What you choose to wear can make a difference in whether you will be noticed—I guess that could be good or that could be bad. It's a choice and a chance—are you willing to take it?

Second, location: There are a few locations that seem to be prime target areas. Parking lots, especially at retail stores, parking garages, and public restrooms are high on the list (probably because of the high number of women who frequent them). However, sometimes it's just being in the wrong "any-place" at the wrong time.

ALERT

We have to live our lives. I would never suggest that we stop going to the grocery store or mall. However, knowing that these areas are attractive to predators, use caution. Look around, and be aware of who or what is around you. If you are returning to your car and you feel uncomfortable, go back and ask a friend or security guard to walk with you.

It Happened

Sam was working in Salt Lake City and since her parents lived close by, she began going to their apartment to visit and eat lunch every day. On this particular day, her parents were not going to be home and Sam, having a key, decided to eat lunch at their apartment anyway. When she pulled into their parking lot, she noticed two men in a parked car staring at her which made her very uncomfortable. CHOICE? Being hungry, she passed her discomfort off as silly and got out of her car and began walking toward the apartment building. The two men also got out of their car and began to follow her. Noticing this, she walked faster, which caused the men to walk faster also. CHOICE? Realizing that she was in danger, she began running. She knew she didn't have time to get to her parents' apartment and unlock their door before the men would catch up with her so she grabbed the first doorknob she came to and ran into a "stranger's" apartment, slamming the door and locking it behind her.

Luckily for Sam, the apartment door she tried was not locked and the woman in the apartment, though stunned at the intrusion, was helpful. (However lucky it was for Sam, anyone could have run into that apartment—keep your doors locked!)

 If you feel uncomfortable, for any reason or for no apparent reason at all, alter your plans.

ALERT

SAFETY TIP:
When walking/jogging or just going from place to place, walk broadly around or away from doorways, bushes, walls, or alleys which you could be pulled into.

Third, isolated and accessible: Who would seem like a better target than a girl walking to her car in a mall parking lot? A girl walking to her car in a mall parking lot with no one else around!

ALERT The bottom line is: Go with a friend rather than alone if possible. If you have to travel alone, take every precaution available to you such as:

- Be alert (notice who and what is around you).
- Use caution.
- Portray confidence.
- Go in the daytime.
- Park in well-lit public spots if you have to go at night.
- Ask someone to walk you to your car if you feel uncomfortable.

It Happened

A woman related a situation to me where she had to visit a business that was "out of the way." In order to access the building, she had to park in an area that was pretty far away, and it would be after dark when she returned. CHOICE? Therefore, she parked in a "no parking" spot right in front of the door, figuring she would rather take her chances with a ticket than walk through a dark, isolated parking lot alone.

ALERT I'm not saying you should break the law, but if you feel uncomfortable about a situation, act on your feelings! You should not be afraid to take any precaution that would help you feel safer.

> **SAFETY TIP:**
> Whenever I am faced with isolation in a remote area, I carry my pepper spray (which is always in my purse) in my hand with my index finger on the trigger. I don't do that in an everyday situation, but when isolated, extra precaution is advisable.

Fourth, distracted: Being distracted gives a predator the element of surprise. Many things can distract you such as: talking to your friends, carrying a baby, holding hands with a child, carrying packages, talking on the cell phone, looking for your keys, searching for your car, etc. Unfortunately, these distractions make you less likely to notice your surroundings, thus making you an easier target.

 ALERT Being aware that distractions could make you an easier target should help you remember to use caution. You cannot afford to have tunnel vision. You must be alert to your surroundings even if your attention is drawn away at times. Some distractions cannot be helped, but some can be avoided.

- Have your keys ready in hand as you walk across a parking lot.
- Remember where your car is (write it down if you always forget).
- Do not talk on a cell phone while strolling along.
- Do not wear headphones while jogging, walking, or riding on public transportation (you are giving up one of your senses—your hearing).
- Do not fall asleep while riding public transportation.

Fifth, appearing easy to control: In the wild, a predatory animal will attack those animals which appear most vulnerable. Slow, lame, or less robust animals will make a much easier target for such predators. Human predators "hunt" for their victims in the same way. A female who seems timid and less confident in her mannerisms will be a more likely target.

ALERT If you look timid, weak, or "willing to please," you will be a more appealing target to a predator. To combat this, carry yourself with confidence—back straight, head up, sturdy step, quick pace, eyes alert meeting the eyes of those around you, know exactly where you are going, have your keys ready, and be aware of your surroundings. Assertive body language is a factor that can eliminate you from becoming a prospective victim. Any hint that you may not be an easy target greatly enhances your chance of being passed over by a predator.

It Happened

One night a friend and I were in a motel in Chicago. Wanting ice, we headed across the parking lot to the manager's room to ask where the ice machine was. Halfway across the parking lot we noticed three men coming out of a bushy area and following us. My friend kept asking me, "What do we do?—What do we do?" CHOICE? I told her to keep walking briskly and confidently. We made it to the manager's office and found out that the ice was just around the corner. CHOICE? If I had been smart, I would have asked him or someone else to walk us back to our hotel room. Because I wasn't so smart, and maybe a little too self-assured, I looked out of the glass doors, didn't see the men, and basically dismissed the thought that they were actually following us. That was a mistake. (Act on your feelings—more in chapter 6.)

We went around the corner into the little laundry room where the ice machine was and got our ice. As we turned to leave, one of the men stepped into the entry-way of the ice room. His eyes were glazed, his pants unzipped, and in order to leave the room we would have to squeeze past him. CHOICE? I picked up the ice bucket, took my friend's arm, and marched right up to him. I looked him squarely in the eyes and said, "Excuse me please!" as we walked right past him back to our room.

Although I did not do the right thing at first by not asking the manager to escort us back to our room, I definitely did the right thing later by asserting myself—looking him straight in the eyes in the laundry room.

ALERT
Predators are cowards and they are looking for an easy target. Lowering your eyes as you meet people will portray you as weak. Always look people in the eyes with confidence. A friend who used to work at the Utah State Penitentiary told me that in her training she was told that the inmates had admitted that women who did not look into their eyes were their prime targets. She also told me of this experience that she had:

It Happened

Char had decided to do a 5-mile walk around the track at the local hospital. Unknown to her, that very day an assailant had attacked and molested a woman in the local grocery store parking lot. While the police were responding to that call, he attacked another woman at another grocery store parking lot. He left that scene and molested a third woman who had just given birth at the local Community Hospital. The man then ran out of the hospital and not being able to get to his car, stole a bike and took off.

Here we pick up Char's story. As she was walking along the track, along came a man on a bicycle. CHOICE? She looked at him, met his eyes, said "Hi," and kept walking. She said his face looked troubled and uncertain, as if he was hesitant, but then he went on his way. As the scenario played out, she then saw the man urgently trying to get his car started in the hospital parking lot (she later found out the police had tampered with the car, making it impossible to start). As she walked through the parking lot to her own car, the scene exploded with sirens, cars, and officers as this man was apprehended and taken into custody.

The next day she found out that the man she had met on the bike was the same assailant that had molested the three women that very same day. Because she had worked at the state penitentiary, she was well aware of how to "meet" a stranger. She is confident that the fact that she looked him in the eyes, and even spoke to him, took her out of the running to be his fourth victim that day.

Sixth, environment: The environment that you surround yourself in can make a difference in your likelihood of being targeted. Any place alcohol, drugs, and lewd behavior are present (sound like a high school or college party?), your chances of being a target increase. This is due to the fact that in these environments there are a large number of people not in full control of themselves. In addition, you may not be in control of yourself either.

It Happened

Jessica, an LDS young woman, accompanied some non-LDS friends to a party where she knew there would be drinking and drugs. She went just to hang out and be the "designated driver" to get her friends home safely.

At the party, she drank a soda while the others got drunk. Several boys kept eyeing her and at some point during the evening, one of them slipped a drug into her soda. The next thing she remembered was lying naked in the shower, with cold water spraying on her. Her drunk friends had finally found her in the bedroom, having been raped multiple times, and took her into the shower to try to awaken her.

Jessica learned the hard way the risk of placing yourself in such a dangerous situation. Some of you may think that you can walk the fine line between a party life style and Church membership. Many young women feel that it's okay to hang around their school friends who are into the party scene on Friday and Saturday nights because they are not "participating" in the drinking or drugs.

 You must be aware that putting yourself in an environment that caters to the loss of inhibition is extremely dangerous. Such an environment promotes predatorial tendencies in some, and desensitizes others to danger. In other words, there is a good chance that those who could become assailants will become assailants, and those who could become victims will become victims.

Remember, we're talking about the defense of our virtue, our self-esteem, and our lives. If for any reason or no reason at all you feel uncomfortable going to a party, a friend's home, a dance, a date, etc.—don't go!

That leads me to give you the best reason for not placing yourself in these kinds of situations, even if you aren't participating. The Holy Ghost is the greatest gift you have. If you choose to put yourself into these environments, you will have to leave the Spirit (your buddy) at the door. He cannot enter. Since He cannot stay with you if you choose to drive Him away, you have lost His companionship and therefore, His guidance and protection. That puts you on your own and that is a lonely and dangerous place to be! If the Spirit wouldn't go there, neither should you!

Remember:

- You can interrupt the Assault Pattern and avoid being a target by being alert to your surroundings.
- You may be female, but you can make important choices that will reduce or eliminate the chance that you will ever become a target.
- Use caution, be alert, and avoid distractions such as cell phones and headphones.
- Use assertive body language, and move with confidence.
- Always look people in the eyes.
- Stay away from environments which promote the loss of inhibition. (You may find you lose a lot more than that.)

Chapter Five

Choose to Pass the Test

"Act as if what you do makes a difference. It does."
—William James

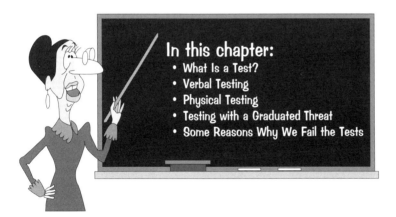

In this chapter:
- What Is a Test?
- Verbal Testing
- Physical Testing
- Testing with a Graduated Threat
- Some Reasons Why We Fail the Tests

What Is a Test?

The second step in the assault pattern is "test." After a predator has zeroed in on a target, he will likely test her to make sure he can intimidate and control her. (Sometimes this step is skipped if an assailant thinks he automatically has an upper edge—perhaps he finds a woman alone and isolated; this may be good enough for him.)

However, most often he will use one or more of the forms of testing listed below to see just how compliant his targeted victim will be. Let me show you what I mean:

It Could Happen

A predator may see a girl at a skating rink and observe that she seems a little more timid than the other girls (target). He may want to find out just how easily he could control her by skating very close beside her (test). Her reaction to this stranger skating uncomfortably close to her will tell him a lot. CHOICE? If she just looks embarrassed, he will definitely continue the testing stage. If she forcefully tells him to "please move," he will most probably go off in search of a new victim, one that he can intimidate easily.

 Men most often rape for control or revenge. If a sexual predator thinks he can control you, you will likely become his victim. Did I mention that these people are cowards? If you give him any indication that you may not be an easy victim, you will probably stop his assault in the testing stage.

Let's look at the different ways an assailant might test his victim:

Verbal Testing

Many assailants use verbal intimidation only. This intimidation is designed to unnerve, agitate, stun, and paralyze you with shock and fear.

1) Sweet talk, unnatural talk, or a combination: On a less sinister level, you might hear this kind of talk coming from a group of men who, because they are in a group of their peers, feel like they can take inappropriate liberties. They might make kissing noises,

whistle, or catcall to a girl as she passes by—anything to annoy and frustrate her. Sweet talk such as, "Shake it," "Work it girl," and "Um, um, I like the way you move" are typical from these groups of men who are getting a power-rush at your expense. It's sort of a male bravado thing—they are doing it more to impress their peers than anything. Though these comments are in fact an assault on you, there is often no violence intended. In this kind of situation the best thing you can do is not allow them to visibly see that you are flustered. Portray confidence, and get out of earshot as quickly as possible.

However, violent predators will use these same words to stun and intimidate you. Sayings such as, "Mmm, I like the way you move" or "You smell so good" from a group of men at a work site is irritating and embarrassing, but when they are directed at you, one-on-one, from a stranger, they can have a paralyzing effect. For many assailants, these words intimidate their victims just as easily as a weapon.

 One of the reasons these words are so paralyzing is because **ALERT** we don't know quite how to react. They play upon our emotions and even though your instincts tell you that this person is dangerous, the "nice" person in you doesn't want to be rude to someone who is saying "flattering things." This contradiction in sympathies has a paralyzing effect. The way their words are used are not flattering. They are demeaning and are intended to hurt and belittle you.

 If you recognize that these words are used by a predator to test his victim, you can hear the words for what they are, an assault on you, testing you to see if he can control you. You will be able to confidently show your assailant that his words will not intimidate you by saying such things as, "Get away from me," "Bug off," or "Leave me alone!" Remember, you don't say

these words as an apology or question. You say them firmly, looking him straight in the eye and making your point clear. You will not be intimidated by him or anyone else!

Another ploy a predator might use is to change his voice into sounding unnatural. He may make it baby-like, mocking, deep, menacing, or bizarre. His intent is to take you off guard and basically give you the creeps. When someone talks, we expect to hear a normal voice. When that sound is altered, it can throw us off balance and create a paralyzing fear within us.

It Happened

Donna left her boyfriend's apartment and headed for the parking lot. As she got off the elevator and began walking to her car, she had a million things on her mind. Suddenly she was brought to attention by a man's voice saying, "Excuse me." Turning, she found herself face to face with a man she hadn't even noticed. Suddenly, he changed the tone of his voice from normal to a high-pitched baby voice and said, "You're afraid of me?" He then dropped his voice as he walked toward her and said in an eerie deep tone, "I'm armed." Back in his falsetto, he taunted, "You don't believe me, do you?" Then, in a deep voice, "You should." **CHOICE?**

Donna abruptly turned and ran. Reaching the stairs, she began racing back toward the apartment. Midway up the second flight of stairs, the stranger lunged at her from behind, grabbing her as he landed on top of her. It was then that she noticed a long serrated blade at his side. **CHOICE?** Donna started screaming for her life and shrieking, "David, David!" Deterred by the noise and the attention it would bring, Donna's attacker left abruptly.

 First of all, Donna should have been more aware of her **ALERT** surroundings. Because she was distracted and her mind "elsewhere," her attacker was able to take her by surprise. However, when her assailant tried to verbally intimidate her through his range of eerie voices, rather than freezing and complying, she resisted by running and screaming. Donna made enough noise that her would-be attacker slithered off. Assailants don't like noise drawing attention to their attacks (more on that in chapter 7).

2) Threats: Sometimes testing is done with the upfront threat of harm.

It Happened

Jean was leaving her office one night. Knowing that she would be leaving after dark and alone, she had parked her car under a light. She walked confidently to her car, and began to unlock it. Around the car a man approached and said menacingly, "I'm going to kill you." CHOICE? Without missing a beat, Jean replied firmly, "If you do, then I'll kill you right back!" This stunned her assailant and off he went.

ALERT Jean was able to stop the assault in the testing stage because she did not cower when her assailant threatened to kill her. She showed him by her retort that she would not be intimidated and would not be an easy victim for him. Have I mentioned that predators are cowards?

3) Vulgarity: This form of verbal testing can be anything from making graphic comments about your body parts to using lewd and foul language in general. Profanity is used so frequently in our society that we have become desensitized to it. However, when profanity is directed at you, in a menacing way, it can achieve the effect your assailant is aiming for.

ALERT You must prepare yourself for the foulest possible things anyone could ever say because if a predator is using this type of verbal threat, he will use words and statements meant to shock and intimidate you. I'm not going to write out things that could be said, but you can bet that the worst you can come up with will be the mildest your assailant can dish out.

Therefore, if this type of testing is ever used on you, remember that words are just words. The mouth they are coming out of belongs to a coward that you will not allow to control you.

4) Familiarity: Your assailant may use statements that show he knows something about you such as, "I liked your hair better long," "John isn't good enough for you," or "Are you going back to your Grandma's house soon?" In this manner, he is telling you that he has been watching you. Coming upon a stranger and having him tell you something personal about yourself is bone-chilling, and of course your assailant is counting on this familiarity to shock and stun you. This predator is a stalker. Following a potential victim is part of his game. Having zeroed in on his target, he gets a power-rush by following and studying her. Then, when he feels like it, he uses that knowledge to test his victim, fully expecting to intimidate her into compliance with his demands.

ALERT Once again, any sign of weakness on your part will give your assailant confidence to continue his assault. You must recognize that this is a form of testing which you have power to overcome just like any other form. The fact is, it is very intimidating to realize someone has been watching you and knows something personal about you, but it doesn't change the fact that it is still a test and you can pass it. Your assailant is playing a game. He isn't quite sure he can control you yet—you must show him that he can't. Showing the same confidence in your body language and your verbal responses as you would to any other "test" will discourage him from continuing his assault.

> **SAFETY TIP:**
> In some extreme cases of stalking, you may need police involvement to control the situation. If someone tests you in this familiar way—and continues to harass you even after you have given him every indication that you will not cave in to his intimidation—he may have zeroed in on you and only you no matter what. This kind of stalking will require help from the authorities.

ALERT You cannot dictate what is said or not said to you. All you can do is control your reaction to it. This testing ploy is used by two types of predators: those simply trying to unnerve you "for the fun of it," and those with the intent of causing you physical harm. Your response will either stop the assault or perpetuate your vulnerability.

You've been taught in church and school to know ahead what you will do if someone offers you cigarettes, alcohol, drugs, etc. You need the same preparation for your personal defense. Remember your motto: Be Prepared! Think about it now; prepare yourself to not only recognize verbal testing, but plan how you will react to put a stop to an assault in this testing stage. Remember, words are just words. There is a coward lurking behind the mouth and you are not intimidated by cowards!

Physical Testing

1) Touch: You may think physical testing includes an attacker grabbing your arm, tackling you from behind, or choking you. Later in this book, I will teach you how to physically defend against these

attacks. However, you also need to realize that in the testing stage an assailant could easily grab your breasts, rip your shirt open, or put his hand up your skirt or down your pants. Such physical attacks are intended to stun and paralyze you into submission. His aim could be just for his own jollies, or it could be to test your potential as his next rape victim. Either way, he is assessing your compliance.

It Happened

A woman entered a crowded subway car and found no place to sit. Taking one of the handles, she consigned herself to standing. Shortly after the car began moving, a man began to fondle her breasts. **CHOICE? The** woman, too embarrassed to say anything, did nothing and he continued his assault all the way to her stop.

ALERT
This assailant was counting on the fact that the woman would be too embarrassed to make a scene, and would therefore allow him to get his jollies. In this case, he guessed right. Too intimidated to turn and slap him, too scared to move, and too embarrassed to make a scene by yelling at him, she cared more about pleasing him than defending her own dignity.

2) Weapons: Many times I'm asked, "So what should I do if he has a weapon?" My response is, "Resist whether he has a weapon or not!" This is a controversial position to take. Certainly your immediate danger is greater if you resist when a weapon is involved, but it will still be your choice. If you submit to his demands, your choices will soon become non-existent. Remember, most of the time, any sign of resistance will automatically take you out of the running as an appealing target.

It Happened

A woman was confronted in her hallway by a man holding a knife. He demanded that she take him to her apartment. CHOICE? The woman flatly refused and the man, unnerved by her resistance, turned and ran. The woman later found out that this man had assaulted more than a hundred women. Her composure and resistance had sent him off to find an easier victim.

ALERT Think of it this way, if an assailant threatens you with bodily harm from his weapon if you do not submit to his demands (such as: go with him, stop screaming, get in the car, etc.), what do you think the chances are that he won't use it if you do submit? In other words, if he has a weapon, the chances are good that he will use it—if not now, later when you are under his complete control; tied up and at his disposal.

This is a personal decision for everyone and one that you need to make now while you can think rationally. The chances are pretty good that if you resist, weapon or not, your assailant will move on to an easier target. Why? Because if he is using his weapon to intimidate you into going with him, his intentions are to take you someplace private where he can have complete control over you. It is not his intention to shoot you there on the spot. (If that was his intention, he would have done it already.) Your resistance will force him to do just that—shoot you on the spot—or go find another target on which to carry out his full assault plan. You will have interrupted his plans.

However, if your resistance doesn't send him off and instead he turns his weapon on you, it is my personal choice to be shot or stabbed right there in public. I would choose to make a huge scene and a lot of noise, bringing all kinds of attention to myself and my assailant, instead of allowing him to take me to a secluded area, where I would be under his complete control and where he could torture and rape me with no one to hear my cries. (More on this in chapter 10.)

SAFETY TIP:
If you resist an assailant who is holding a gun, running may be your best option.

- A bullet can only go in a straight line.
- Run in a curved line away from your assailant and toward safety.
- At a distance of nine feet, criminals only hit their victims 4 out of 100 times (see Richard J. Machowicz and Patrick D. Malone in Dana Hudepohl, "15 Ways to Save Your Life," *Glamour*, August 2000, p.255).

If you cannot run or there is no safe place to run to, fainting may be your next best option. Drop to the ground as dead weight, pretending to faint. Your assailant will either have to leave you there or try to get you to go with him. If he tries to drag you someplace or get you into a car, the chances are that he will have to put his weapon aside. This would be your chance to fly into a RAGE and stage your own active resistance. (More in chapter 7.)

Testing with a Graduated Threat

Testing with a graduated threat means that you have some kind of relationship with the assailant. It could be a conversation with someone you just met or it could be that you've known him for a long time. This relationship typically begins friendly and impersonal, but over time (either minutes or months), it escalates into a situation that is uncomfortable and/or dangerous.

It could take minutes: This kind of testing is used often at a bus stop, in line at an amusement park, or at the airport, mall, or on a subway. It could be used anywhere you are in close proximity with someone for a relatively short amount of time.

It Could Happen

You're waiting for your mom to pick you up from the mall. A man standing nearby begins to make conversation with you. He is friendly, asking casual questions, but within a few minutes his questions become more personal, such as, "What is your name?" "How old are you?" "Where do you live?" As his questions take a more personal turn, you notice that he's moved uncomfortably close to you. CHOICE?

You could walk away, or you could use verbal resistance saying something like: "You're sitting too close to me," or, "Your questions aren't appropriate," or, "Please move," or "Bug off!" You could also fidget, squirm, and do nothing.

ALERT If you choose to fidget, squirm, and do nothing, this man will either annoy and embarrass you as long as he wants to, or if his intentions are violent, he will move into the next stage of his assault which is to attack. I think you can imagine by now what walking away or verbally resisting will do for you in this situation—yep, you're right, it will interrupt his testing tactics and disappoint him terribly. He will most probably move on to an easier target.

It Happened

Melanie was at the bus stop with a friend. She noticed a man walking back and forth and staring at her. Eventually he began talking to her and before long, she was uncomfortable with his questions. CHOICE?

Not knowing quite what to do, she tried to ignore him. When the bus came, the two girls quickly entered and the man got on also. He edged his way towards her and, standing along side her, took hold of her hand. **CHOICE?** Melanie was so embarrassed and shocked, she didn't know what to do. Trying to indicate that he was holding her hand to her friend, she once again ignored the man. At the next stop, her friend, understanding Melanie's predicament, got off and pulled Melanie with her.

ALERT If you allow this testing to go unresisted, you will become a victim. You may be a victim for someone getting a kick out of your discomfort, or you may be a victim for someone with more sinister plans in mind. Walking away or saying, "No!" in whatever manner is convenient will put a damper on this would-be assailant. If you choose to say, "Bug off," do not say it as an apology. Say, "Bug off!" Say it with your mouth, your eyes, and your body language. This jerk has no right to be making you uncomfortable.

"Please help me": Another form of graduated testing which takes only minutes is the "please help me" ploy. In this ploy, your assailant acts helpless in some way. Perhaps he needs directions, he lost his dog, he has a flat tire, or he can't carry all of his packages. You name it, it has been used. He is testing you to see if you are one of those nice people who will help him even if you feel uncomfortable. In this way an assailant will lure his victim closer to him, his car, or into an isolated area.

ALERT You can be cautiously polite. You can talk to someone and even give him directions. However, make sure the conversation flows on your terms without bending to any of his personal demands, no matter how innocent they seem. If this makes you feel a little rude, it's OK! (Better safe than sorry— or in this case better rude then sorry.) If you are uncomfortable for any reason or for no reason at all, leave the situation.

"Please help me" ploy #2: A predator could just hobble along obviously needing help but not asking for it, waiting until a nice female offers to lend him assistance. In this way, his victim would never suspect him of evil intentions; he's just a nice man needing help. His attack will take her totally by surprise.

It Happened

The notorious serial killer Ted Bundy used the "helpless ploy" to murder many young women. He used fake casts and splints as props as he feigned a broken arm or leg. In one case he is believed to have targeted a woman leaving a library. Wearing a splint on one hand and a sling on the opposite arm, Bundy dropped a load of books while grimacing in "pain." CHOICE? Predictably, the concerned woman probably asked, "Do you need help?" Without suspecting what was in store for her, the woman is believed to have helped Bundy carry his books to his car, which of course was in a dark and isolated area.

ALERT If you wouldn't ordinarily walk with someone you don't know to an isolated place, don't do it just because they seem to need help. So if someone wearing a cast dropped some books, should you just ignore him? That's a tough question. You don't want to become the type of person so self-absorbed or paranoid that you can't help people. Most situations are legitimate, but what you must do is use caution. There is never a need to be alone in any way with someone you help. You should never feel like you have to do anything that is even the least bit uncomfortable. Tune into your feelings and if the situation seems improbable or you feel uncomfortable in any way or for any reason, get out.

Hours, days, weeks, or longer: Sometimes this gradual testing can span a length of time. In these cases, the assailant is someone you've known for a while, not just a chance meeting somewhere. It could be someone you think of as a friend and feel pretty comfortable around. Your tip-off here is when your "friend" begins making you uncomfortable, even if it's just a little bit.

That is usually the beginning of a graduated assault. The little bits of inappropriate speech or touching that your "friend" has begun using around you will become more and more blatant over time until it becomes a full-fledged assault or you have put a stop to it. For example:

It Happened

A woman in one of my classes told me about a man that she worked with who at first was very nice and friendly. As weeks went by, his friendliness became more and more inappropriate. CHOICE? Eventually he began leering and rolling his tongue when he saw her. CHOICE? She talked to her husband about it and despite his desire to "take care of the guy," she decided to handle it herself.

The next time he gave her the stare and rolled his tongue at her, she got right up in his face with a pair of scissors, pointed them at his mouth, and yelled, "If you ever do that to me again, I'll cut your tongue out!" In doing so, she used her eyes, her voice, and her stance to effectively portray her demeanor. (In other words, she really let him have it!)

He never bothered her again, but was eventually fired from that job due to sexual harassment complaints.

ALERT

You have to "nip it in the bud," so to speak. Stand up for yourself as soon as you feel uncomfortable. The sooner the better—you'll save yourself a lot of uneasiness and worry over what to do. If you make the decision right now that you will never let someone take advantage of you this way, your response if someone begins making small inappropriate comments will be immediate. You might say, "Don't talk to me like that," or "You are pushing our friendship—I won't be talked to like that." The first time someone tries rolling his tongue at you, just say something like, "Don't ever roll your tongue at me again!" This would probably take care of the problem (even without the scissors).

Your assailant would find out right upfront that he is not going to get his power-rush at your expense, and he'd likely turn his inappropriate attentions to someone else. Unfortunately, many girls don't understand that they have the power within themselves to say "No!" to these inappropriate situations, and therefore they are taken advantage of.

It Happened

Marci (not her real name) was at a party. Throughout the night, a certain young man paid a lot of attention to her. At first he was friendly and they were having a good time. As the night drew on, his attention became unwanted, his comments crude, and his suggestions inappropriate. By the end of the night, Marci wanted nothing to do with him.

It just so happened that when it was time to go home, this young man and others had asked to ride with the friend Marci had come with. After they all piled into the car, there were no seats left. In front of her crowd of peers, the young man insisted that she sit on his lap in the back seat. **CHOICE?**

Not wanting to sit on his lap, but not wanting to make a scene, she hesitantly consented and took a seat on his lap. She was in for a ride home from "Hades." The young man took advantage of her location and reluctance to make a scene by fondling and invading her with his hands. **CHOICE?** She endured his assault until the car pulled up in front of his house. Laughing and joking about it, he and his friend got out of the car and left Marci with a crude gesture. Marci rode the rest of the way home feeling raped and ashamed.

So how could Marci have prevented this from happening? She already distrusted this young man and felt uncomfortable around him. There were two pivotal times for her to choose. Once she made the wrong choice by sitting on his lap, she still had the choice to stop what he was doing. Why didn't she?

Some Reasons We Fail the Tests

Remember, a predator tests his target to make sure she will be easy for him to control. He wants to be successful in his planned assault. If you fail his test, he will be confident that you will make an easy victim, and will submit to his demands with little or no resistance. Failure often means you are:

- Too nice to risk offending someone, even a stranger.
- Too embarrassed to make a scene or call attention to yourself.
- Too flattered by his attention to see his intentions.

 Regardless of the reason, all who fall into one of these definitions end up as victims.

Too nice: Can you ever be too nice? Unfortunately you can if you are inadvertently submitting to a predator who, recognizing your kindness, takes advantage of you because of it.

It Happened

Doris was approached by a man who lived in her neighborhood. Telling her he had a car accident a few years back and couldn't work, he asked her if he could mow her lawn for $10.00. She agreed to let him do the work and also to the amount he would charge. After she agreed, he told her that in order to mow the lawn, he first needed his medicine, asking for payment up front. **CHOICE?** She hesitantly agreed and paid him the $10.00. He left (to get his "medicine") and eventually came back and mowed the lawn. Throughout the summer, he mowed her lawn a few more times, always asking for payment upfront.

Months later, he approached her again, asking if he could rake her leaves for $20.00, again requesting the payment upfront. **CHOICE?** Doris agreed and paid him the $20.00. This time after taking the money and going to get his "medicine," he never came back to do the job. A couple of weeks later he came back, this time asking for $50.00, telling her he was sorry and would make up the work he had missed, but he was really sick and needed his medicine first. **CHOICE?** Doris didn't really trust him this time, but gave him $50.00 anyway because—well just because she was nice! The man never showed up to do the promised work.

ALERT This predator was looking for someone who was nice enough not to turn him away, even when he had not followed through on his promised work. As of this date, he now has $70.00 of unearned money. This pattern could easily have continued, except Doris realized that this man was preying on her sympathies. She will not be his victim again.

Too embarrassed: Being too embarrassed is a huge problem for many girls. Some of it has to do with self-esteem, some of it personality, and some of it is that you just don't know what to do in an uncomfortable situation. Any way you look at it, the bottom line is that some girls are too embarrassed to cause a scene or call attention to themselves. They may even think that people will think they don't have the right to complain or that they are making a big deal out of nothing.

It Could Happen

You are sitting on the school bus and a boy sits next to you. He is not your boyfriend and not even a friend. During the ride home, he puts his hand on your thigh. You are utterly stunned and don't know what to say or do. CHOICE? He begins to rub your thigh with a mocking smile on his face.

ALERT This boy has targeted you as someone who would be too embarrassed to say anything that would call attention to yourself. Because he feels like you won't do anything about it, he's having a little power rush at your expense. Your life may not be in danger, but you are the victim of a predator who is attacking your dignity. Calling attention to the situation is exactly what you must do! All it would take is to say, "Get your hands off of me!" with your voice, eyes and body language, and you would be his victim no more.

Once you speak up for yourself this way, never back down! Maybe this young man would act like you are crazy saying, "What's your problem?" However, his attempt at a cover up doesn't matter. You know what happened, the Lord knows what happened, and the fact that this young man is trying to play it off at your expense doesn't change the truth. Your self-respect is precious; never apologize for keeping it.

It Happens

I've been told by young women that some high school guys are notorious for feeling like they can say anything to a girl and it's "OK." Some guys take advantage of their popularity and status in school to demean or insult girls, usually to look "macho" in front of their friends. They are predators in their own right, absorbing a power-rush at your expense. This "gang mentality" gives these guys a feeling of invincibility.

ALERT Resist them the same way you would resist a complete stranger that treated you that way. Look them squarely in the eyes and tell them what you think! You might even use an elbow in the stomach if the occasion warrants it.

> **GANG MENTALITY:** Some people who are part of a group that is bonded together by loyalty, camaraderie, or a cause, will do something with this group they would never do as individuals. This is called "gang mentality." Usually, the deed will be stupid, dangerous, or immoral (i.e. inappropriate comments, rioting, looting, cross burning, lynch mobs, gang rape, etc.)

Too flattered: Every girl likes to be flattered, right? Well, true compliments, yes, but flattery as a lure? No! The problem is that many girls don't know the difference. They don't recognize "luring-flattery" when they hear it because they're too flattered!

It Happened

Some teenage girls were at an arcade together. While they were playing around, a stranger began paying special attention to one of the girls. He used a lot of flattery to try to lure her off with him and away from her friends. **CHOICE?** The other girls could see right through the guy's advances, and would not let their friend be alone with him. She, on the other hand, was not used to such attention and became caught up with his flattery. She could not understand her friends' concern.

ALERT Knowing that predators will use flattery to prey on those who are less confident and easily swayed, analyze yourself to determine if you would be a likely victim. If a guy was truly interested in you as a person, not as a victim, he would respect the fact that you were with friends and join in the camaraderie. If his sole purpose was to get you alone with him, he probably has inappropriate intentions.

Arm yourself with the determination that you will never fall into these traps. Practice verbal resistance in front of the mirror if it helps. Stand there and just say "no!" using your voice, eyes, and body language. You're probably pretty good at talking to your brothers or sisters that way; now transfer all that good know-how and energy into defending your body and spirit.

SAFETY TIP:

If you ever have a question as to whether someone's flattery is real or being used to lure you into going somewhere or doing something that could be dangerous to your body or spirit, step back and tap into what you're really feeling. Don't let flattery cloud your common sense. If you are even the slightest bit uncomfortable, you can be sure the Spirit is trying to break through the cloud of garbage your flatterer is shoveling out in an attempt to lure you into something you will be sorry for. You owe it to yourself to recognize that still small voice, even if it is very small, and trust it. Remember, the Spirit will guide, and you can stop this assault in the testing stage.

Your resistance can help others. You may think that you are alone in carrying the burden of unwanted remarks and gestures. However, if an assailant is making you uncomfortable, the chances are pretty good that other girls are getting the same treatment from him as well.

It Happened

A woman in one of my classes told me about a restaurant she worked at where the manager, at first friendly, began making comments that were not appropriate. CHOICE? Eventually his comments were so extreme she couldn't take it any more and she told him to stop! As the word spread that she had handled the situation, more and more of the servers found the courage to tell him to stop also. He was eventually fired for sexual harassment.

ALERT

Don't be afraid to stop this kind of treatment immediately. Your resistance could give courage and help to someone else who is in a troubling situation. Do not be afraid to stand up for your self-esteem! You will not only help yourself, but you could be helping others, too.

Remember:

- Predators test you to see if you will submit to their demands.
- You cannot dictate what is said to you. All you can do is control your reaction to it.
- Resisting an assailant, especially if he has a weapon, is a personal decision and one you need to make now, while you can think rationally.
- Emphasize your verbal resistance. Say "No!" with your voice, your eyes, and your body language.
- Recognize and choose to stop any kind of assault in the testing stage, regardless of the embarrassment.
- Your self-respect is precious; never apologize for keeping it.
- You must be more interested in your own personal defense than in pleasing a stranger.

Chapter Six

Choose to Avoid Becoming a Victim

"If it is to be it is up to me."
–William H. Johnsen

In this chapter:
- Your First Line of Defense
- Use Caution and Common Sense
- Accept the Possibility That This Could Happen to You
- Listen to the Spirit
- Get Out!

Your First Line of Defense

Avoiding a physical confrontation is your first line of defense and the best personal defense skill you can have. Though it may not sound like something you'd find a super hero doing, it is guaranteed to keep you safe every time you use it—and that is your goal. Remember, any time there is a physical confrontation, someone will get hurt and that someone will very likely be you. However, if you avoid a confrontation altogether, no one gets hurt.

Use Caution and Common Sense

It would be redundant to talk a lot more about this. We've been talking about caution (being alert) throughout this whole book. However, I would like to make a statement about the obvious. Most of you already know a lot of personal defense tips such as:

- Lock your car doors.
- Use the buddy system.
- Park in well-lighted areas.
- Look in your car before entering.
- Don't give out personal information.
- Don't pick up hitchhikers and don't hitchhike.
- Don't stop at the scene of a breakdown. Call for help.
- Lock your doors at home.
- Don't open the door to strangers.

 We could go on and on with lists of safety tips, many of them you've already heard. Now here is my simple statement: Follow every tip you possibly can!

It Happened

One day my clothes dryer was broken, and I needed to borrow a friend's machine. When I asked if I could come over to use it, she said, "Sure, come over anytime because we're going out of town." I questioned, "How will I get in?" Her reply, "Just come on in, we never lock the doors."

 My friend either sounds just like you, or astonishes you. A lot of your attitudes about being cautious depend on the area you live in and the experiences you've had. However, may

I suggest that to think just because nothing has ever happened to you, it never will, is pretty much a "La-La-Land" attitude. Bad things happen. To think "that could never happen to me" might prevent you from taking the very precautions that would ensure it wouldn't. So many times, a little thing such as keeping doors locked would have saved a life.

Accept the Possibility That This Could Happen to You

There are three different attitudes you could have toward your own personal defense. They are:

1) Nothing will happen.
2) Something will happen.
3) Something could happen.

1) Nothing will happen: Time for a reality check. Remember the "La-La-Land" attitude? Some girls think that just because nothing has ever happened to them, nothing ever will. To see the fallacy in this type of thinking, all you need to do is get into a group of girls or women and begin talking about their experiences. You will soon find that at least half of the females in the group (if not more) have experienced an assault of some kind. From take-advantage assault to sexual harassment to an aggravated sexual or physical attack, most women have some kind of story to tell. To think that you will escape completely is dangerous because it stops you from accepting reality. There are two main problems with this attitude:

First, if you think that nothing could ever happen to you, you may take risks and put yourself in dangerous situations. You might ignore warnings from the Spirit and be reckless, go to parties where there is drinking and/or drugs, or you may go out one-on-one with a guy you barely know, even though you're not totally comfortable with him, because of course, you are invincible!

Second, if you think nothing can ever happen to you, and it does, it becomes such a surprise you will be stunned when it happens. In a "paralyzed" state, you will not be able to take the action you need to give yourself a fighting chance. If you have this attitude, you will never accept and apply any of the lessons you are learning in this book. You are putting yourself in danger, hiding like an ostrich with its head in a hole, hoping that no one sees you. You will not be prepared for anything out of the norm and unfortunately, things out of the norm happen whether you think they can or not. If you tend to lean toward this feeling of denial, snap out of it!

2) Something will happen: This is a crippling attitude. To think that something will happen will make you paranoid. This mentality will not allow you to function in everyday life because you will always be afraid of everything and everyone around you.

> Let the fear of danger be a spur to prevent it, he that fears not, gives advantage to the danger.
> -Frances Quarles (1592-1644)

Much in this life is good, and most people you interact with are wonderful. If you live with paranoia, you will never be able to reach your true potential. You will limit yourself and your contacts and you will lose much of what life has to offer.

If you tend to feel paranoid, get on your knees and pray for help. It's not always easy to figure out why we feel a certain way; you may need the Lord's help to overcome those feelings. Remember His message: "Be not afraid, only believe." (Mark 9:23)

3) Something could happen: Accepting the fact that though there is much good in the world, "sometimes bad things happen" is a healthy attitude. Because you understand that fact, you will be able to prepare yourself by being cautious and alert. You will recognize situations and people that make you feel uncomfortable, and you will avoid them.

Only by accepting the fact that something could happen can you be prepared to face it with every advantage. If you are physically attacked by an assailant, you will be ready and able to take the necessary action to give yourself a fighting chance.

Listen to the Spirit

This is my favorite thing to talk about because it is so amazing! Self defense experts call it your heart, feelings, intuition, or gut instincts; religious people call it the Spirit. Let's simply name it for what it is: The Holy Ghost, that personal buddy the Lord has given each of you to guide you through mortality both spiritually and physically.

The Spirit is your best friend, and your personal built-in alarm system. I can't stress enough the value of this gift to your safety. If you will listen to and follow the Spirit, you will keep yourself out of harm's way most of the time.

It Happened

We lived in a very secluded neighborhood in Georgia. The houses, surrounded by trees, were away from the road. I could sit on my porch and never see a soul all day since our neighbors all worked and when they came home late at night they drove right into their garages. I tell you this so you will understand my surroundings.

One day, I decided to go for a walk. As I was coming down the hill toward my home, I noticed a red truck with a trailer parked across the street from my driveway. This was not unusual since those neighbors had their lawn cared for every week by people in this same truck. However, as I approached my driveway and saw a couple of the men standing by the truck, I felt very uneasy. I can't explain it, I just felt like I shouldn't go home. There was no reason for my feeling; the men weren't looking weird, or staring at me, it was just a feeling I had. CHOICE? Therefore, I took a side street and waited until they left before going home.

I wish I could tell you some heroic story about an amazing escape, but I think I just did. I have no idea what would have happened if I had decided to walk past these men on that particular day. It doesn't matter though, because I did what I felt I should, and I'm here today to talk about it.

ALERT

Who knows what would have happened if I had shrugged off the feeling that I shouldn't go home? Maybe nothing would have happened, but maybe something would have. That was a risk I wasn't willing to take.

So often when women who have been assaulted (especially those who have been the victims of date rape) are asked about the attack, they will say something like, "I knew I shouldn't go to that party," "I knew something was wrong," "He made me uncomfortable all night," "I knew I shouldn't go out with him," or "I felt uneasy about being alone with him." Looking back, they could clearly see that what they were feeling was a warning from the Spirit. I've heard it said that "hindsight is 20/20." With the Spirit to guide you, you can have "20/20 foresight" too!

Many times throughout this book, I have said and will say, "If you feel uncomfortable for any reason or for no reason at all, leave, get out, or don't go." This personal alarm system usually gives you warnings through your feelings. It would be nice if a big neon sign popped up and said, "Warning, danger, do not go!" However, most often the Spirit's warnings come as a slight, uneasy feeling, a touch of doubt, or maybe you will be just a little uncomfortable for a minute. When you feel this way, you don't need to give excuses. You just need to change the situation any way that makes you feel comfortable again.

 Way too often we feel uneasy and we tell ourselves that we're being silly or stupid. The silly and stupid part comes when we do not listen to one of the greatest gifts we have. The Spirit gives direction, not explanations. My final words: If you feel something is wrong, it probably is.

In addition, even though you've heard it a million times, here it is again: listen to your parents, whom the Spirit can also direct on your behalf.

I don't think it's uncommon for young women to sometimes want to do things, go places, or hang around people that are not good for them both spiritually and/or physically. This could be because you want to impress a guy that seems interested in you, or you want to be accepted by the "cool" crowd at school, or maybe you move to a new area and want to make friends fast. Whatever your reason, you may want to act on those inclinations (kind of a "natural man syndrome"—study Mosiah 3:19). Your buddy, the Spirit, is there to warn you about following those desires which will lead you down a dangerous path.

Unfortunately, sometimes as a teenager, you can be naive to dangers along that path. Because you want something so badly, you might tune your buddy out. It is at these times that your parents can really help you. Your parents are able to receive promptings from the Spirit on your behalf also. How great is that? Not only can you get your own guidance, you even have back-up.

Listen to, and obey your parents, even when you may not like what they have to say. When you have tuned out the Spirit, and your parents "step up" to guide you, the warnings they give you are going to go against the pull you feel to travel a path that appears fun and exciting. However, if you are serious about your personal safety, you can't ignore the caution and the blessing the Lord gives you in the 5th commandment. He says, "Honour thy father and thy mother" (which would include listen to and obey them). Then comes the blessing: "that thy days may be long upon the land which the Lord thy God giveth thee" (Exodus 20:12).

It sounds to me like the Lord is telling you that He will inspire your parents to help guide you and keep you safe—thereby your "days may be long upon the land." If you listen to their counsel, they can help you stay out of situations that you might not recognize as dangerous.

It Happened

A family member has shared a story from his teen years. He had moved from one town in Montana to another about two hours away. One weekend he was invited by his former group of friends in the town he had moved from to go with them as they celebrated one of their birthdays. He was super excited about going out with them since he hadn't seen them for a while, and he was still trying to make new friends in the town he was living in. The day he was to go with them, his mother, who had been supportive of the outing and glad that her son would be able to see his old friends, began to feel uncomfortable about him going. Eventually, she told David that she just didn't feel like he should go, but she couldn't give him any reason other than she just had a bad feeling about it. CHOICE?

You can imagine the frustration David was feeling. He really wanted to go but he also felt like he should honor his mom's feelings. It was one of those inner battles when you know what you should do, but it is not what you want to do so you have to stew about it for a while. He finally decided to listen to his mother's counsel and not go.

That night, he was feeling sorry for himself, thinking about everything he was missing. However, later, when he learned that the car he would have been riding in had run head-on into another car on a mountain highway, he was so grateful that he had listened to his mother. The accident took the life of one of his friends, a passenger in the other car, and crippled another friend. David is positive that his mother's inspiration saved his life that night.

 Because your parents are older and wiser (I know, *much* older), their minds are not clouded with all the social teenage issues that you have. They can usually see things more clearly than you can. They also love you very much and are privileged to receive inspiration on your behalf.

Get Out!

Simple, yet effective. This, of course, will save you a lot of trouble. If you are cautious, and you are listening to the Spirit, you can walk away, leave the party, or even run. The best way to fend off an assault is to get away from it before it has a chance to happen. This is once again interrupting the assault pattern at the "target/ test" level.

Remember:
- Your first line of defense is to avoid a physical confrontation.
- Follow every safety tip you possibly can.
- Accept the possibility that you could be attacked, and that if you are, you will take action.
- Listen to the Spirit. If you feel like something is wrong, it is.
- The Spirit gives direction, not explanations.
- Listen to your parents. The Spirit will inspire them to guide you.
- The best way to fend off an attack is to get away from it before it has a chance to happen.

Chapter Seven

Choose to Take Action

"In any moment of decision the best thing you can do is the right thing, the next best thing is the wrong thing, and the worst thing you can do is nothing."
—Theodore Roosevelt

In this chapter:
- Attack
- Adrenaline
- RAGE
- Learn to RAGE
- Noise

Attack

The third and final stage in the assault pattern will be an "attack." Most of the time, possibly even 95% of the time, you will stop an assault before it ever reaches the attack stage by following the tips and instruction you have already read in this book. However, the reality is that many women are physically attacked. These attacks occur because either a woman did not stop the assault in the "target/test" stages, or she was just in the wrong place at the wrong time.

Sometimes attacks can come from nowhere. Your assailant could be desperate, crazy, drunk, or on drugs and his attack could have absolutely no rhyme or reason behind it. You may have taken every precaution that you possibly could, but still find yourself in a life-threatening situation.

An attack is not the end of the road, you still have choices. If you find yourself at this point of an assault, it is time to muster all of who you are and take action! You are going to do something about it. You are not going to submit to physical and/or sexual abuse. You will resist until you are free or can resist no longer!

These two girls survived by resisting any way they could. You

It Happened

One evening, three teenagers were hanging out with their friends. Close to midnight, a convicted felon wanted on a rape charge approached the teenagers' car, waving a gun. He forced two of the girls into their car and drove off with it. By dawn an Amber Alert, meant to notify the public about a child abduction, went out over the media and on highway signs. Meanwhile, the teenage girls quietly took a knife they kept in the car and devised a plan to free themselves. Silently, they traced letters on each other's hands to communicate.

When the man stopped the car, one of the girls stabbed him while the other hit him with a bottle. Still, their kidnapper persisted, threatening them with his gun. Tipped off by a motorist who saw the car, police quickly arrived, and shot and killed the kidnapper. Traumatized but safe, the girls went home soon after.

have to be willing to do whatever it takes to get out of any dangerous situation you may be in. There are some things you must know about to prepare yourself now for the possibility of a physical attack.

Adrenaline

If you've ever been scared (and who hasn't), you know the feeling of adrenaline pumping through your body. Adrenaline is an interesting thing, it can make you much stronger than normal, and you usually feel little pain while under its influence. When feeling this adrenaline rush during an attack, you will probably do one of three things:

1) Freeze
2) Panic
3) RAGE (this is what you want to do—read on!)

1) Freeze: It seems crazy to think about, but when adrenaline flows, it can actually have a "freezing" effect on your system. Freezing is a common reaction when you haven't mentally prepared yourself for the potential of an attack.

The fact that women tend to freeze when assaulted is something that assailants count on. It is their "bread and butter," you might say. However, this doesn't have to happen, and won't happen if you are prepared and know that you have choices. Your preparation will help you overcome fear and not let it freeze you into paralysis.

2) Panic: If you haven't prepared yourself for the potential of an attack, adrenaline may cause another reaction in your system, "panic." If you panic, you may run around without purpose or flail your arms and legs aimlessly. When you panic, it does little or no harm to your assailant, and it is absolutely useless in defending your body and/or spirit.

3) RAGE: This is what you want to do! In fact, it's so important I'm going to give it its own section:

RAGE

When adrenaline pumps and you feel a great surge of power, you take that power and channel it into RAGE.

R ighteous
A nger
G iving
E nergy

The difference between RAGE and panic is that RAGE is a controlled power that will give your resistance the fury necessary to overcome an assailant. You can still be a really nice and kind person, and RAGE when it's necessary. RAGE is Righteous Anger Giving you Energy!

It Could Happen

Let's say that your father is a master architect and he has designed a gorgeous home for you and your family to live in. It is your responsibility to keep it clean. Traffic in and out of your home from all the visitors your family has makes it difficult to keep clean. Nevertheless, you work extremely hard, and your father praises you for the immaculate condition in which you've kept it.

Your home is built in a prime business location. Because of this, many people are constantly mulling around your property and you and your father have to work extra hard to keep outsiders away from the house.

One day you leave to run errands, and upon your return, you find the house a disaster. There are all sorts of people walking over the flowerbeds and trying to auction off furniture from your home. A local bank has set up a tent, trying to lure customers in off the streets and there is even a prostitution ring that has set up shop in your father's driveway.

This scenario may seem a bit extreme, but this is like the situation our Savior had to deal with the afternoon that He cast the moneychangers from His Father's temple (Mark 11:15-17). Can you understand why He was so angry? Can you also understand that there can be Righteous Anger Giving Energy (RAGE)? Undoubtedly the Savior felt this RAGE as he discovered what had been done to His Father's house—the temple of God.

Your body is a temple and you are a daughter of God! (One of my daughter's favorite lines: "My body is a temple and you don't have a recommend.") Anyone attempting to defile your temple should fuel this RAGE inside of you! How dare anyone try to hurt your body or spirit! You must feel this commitment to yourself! You must feel that you are special and that no one has the right to offend or hurt you in any way. After you make this commitment to yourself, you will be able to channel all the power and energy that adrenaline will give you into a controlled but furious resistance.

It Happened

A well-known movie star was interviewed on a talk show many years ago. She told about a time when she was an aspiring actress and had come home late one night. As she stepped into her stairwell, a man came out from behind the stairs holding a knife. CHOICE? To paraphrase, she said: "I realized that this man was going to rape me, and I got so mad that I just ran at him and head-butted him in the stomach." He ran off.

 This is what **RAGE** truly is! Instead of letting a frightening situation scare you into freezing or panicking, you channel all of that adrenaline into fury and then you take action.

It Happened

Kelli told me of an incident when she had gone up to visit her parents' cabin. Reaching the door before her husband, she opened it and found a drunken man inside whom she recognized as someone who had worked on the cabin for her parents. He was lying on the couch, and another man was sitting at a table twirling a knife. In addition, two scantily-clad women were mulling around the cabin. The room was filled with smoke, beer cans, and a general stench. CHOICE?

She flew into a RAGE seeing how these people had trashed her family's cabin. She ran over to the drunk, lifted him up by the collar, and yelled in his face, "You and your filthy friends get out of here!" Don't forget, this is one little woman taking on four intruders, two of which were big burly men and one of whom was playing with a knife. The people were so astonished at her fury that they took off in a rush. In fact, they left so quickly that they actually had a car accident on their way down the mountain. Later, Kelli found a semi-automatic gun the intruders had left behind.

She said that after the incident was over she shook uncontrollably for a long time. She had no idea where the RAGE had come from, but she didn't think twice about her feelings as it happened. She was just so incensed that these people were violating her family's cabin that she became a force of fury.

I have to wonder what could have happened if she and her husband had come upon this scene and acted scared or intimidated by these armed intruders.

RAGE is not instinctive to everyone. For some girls this comes very naturally, you instinctively protect yourself. If someone offends, belittles, or tries to take advantage of you, you confront and stop them. You feel that you deserve the best treatment the world has to give, and will not accept anything less. If someone tries to hurt you, they had better watch out. If someone dared attack you, your motto is: This will be the hardest thing you will ever do!

However, for many girls this is not a natural response. You do not stand up for yourselves in general, and are intimidated easily. If you were confronted with a dangerous situation, your natural reaction might be to freeze. Do not worry—you do have fury inside of you and you can learn to channel it into RAGE. Let me teach you how to tap into and adopt this emotion for your own personal defense:

Learn to RAGE!

Go Animal! What is the most ferocious animal you can think of? Do you have one in mind? Okay, now think to yourself, what does this animal look like or sound like? More importantly, what would that animal do if it was cornered by an enemy? Pick your animal and envision it. I'll tell you mine. I am a black panther: glistening black coat, brilliant green eyes, red tongue, shiny white fangs with saliva dripping down, and huge paws with needle sharp claws.

Every time I picture myself as this panther, I picture myself in an absolute fury attacking my enemy. At that point, I am totally focused on my survival, willing to do anything to protect myself.

When you envision yourself as your animal, you must be just as focused. Your ferocious animal will fight on and on until it has overcome its assailant or it can no longer physically resist. It is survival at all costs! This is your secret weapon.

Now you do it. Stop reading right now and visualize the most ferocious animal you can imagine. The more detail you use, the more real it will seem. Think about how it sounds, and how it would move and react if cornered. Do not skip this part of your training! Even if you feel that you have a resistor attitude or personality, don't chance it, create your vision of RAGE now!

Practice your "secret weapon." Picture your animal in your mind, and include all the details. Especially imagine the sound and fury of your animal under attack. As silly as it may feel, practice becoming this animal in your mind or even in the mirror, if it helps. Practice it often, let it become your "secret weapon." Wouldn't an assailant be surprised if he tried to attack you? He would have no idea what was in store for him. If he attacked, you would unleash the "secret weapon" on him that you have been thinking about, practicing, and preparing for just that moment. Your RAGE would explode on this sorry soul and would keep exploding until one of you was no longer attacking.

A way to add fuel to this fire of fury within you is to think about it this way: Suppose you are a mother, big sister, aunt, or you are babysitting a child that you love. What would you do if that child were being attacked? Most women at this point say they would "Tear the attacker apart—full fury!" That is the RAGE you are looking for. Practice it.

Noise

During your RAGING fury, make a lot of noise! When I asked the director of the police academy in a college near my home what he felt was the best thing a woman could do when attacked, he said, "Make a lot of noise." An assailant wants things done his way. His wish is for you to submit to his demands so he can do whatever he wants to you. He does not want attention drawn to himself or you, his victim. He wants you to be a good sport, and quietly allow him total control. A lot of noise can quickly disrupt your attacker's plan. You want to call all the attention in the world to yourself at that very moment. Remember Donna from chapter 5? In the end, it was the noise she was making that unnerved her assailant and sent him packing.

So what is the noise you should make? Absolutely anything! Screaming "No!" is effective. In Tae Kwon Do, we are taught to "Kiap," which is basically a yell—kind of like a battle cry. Any type of loud sound or word that you can shout towards your attacker will throw him off.

Yelling:
- Calls attention to yourself.
- Disorients your attacker.
- Brings more oxygen into your brain and muscles, which will give you more power.
- Helps you focus your power.
- Prevents you from biting your tongue or lips.

Turn into that RAGING animal complete with your "battle cry." Now practice it. You could yell "No!" or "Stop!" or just copy your animal's sound and "Roar!" (my personal favorite). I am very serious about practicing your "battle cry." You need to get used to making this kind of loud noise so you can become comfortable with it.

It Happened

When I began taking Tae Kwon Do, I felt so stupid when I had to do the required kiap with each kick or punch. I felt like everyone in the room would notice me and how dumb I sounded. I heard my pathetic kiap above everyone else's and was sure that I sounded ridiculous.

Believe it or not, the kiap was harder than any of the moves I had to learn for the first little while. However, the more I heard myself shouting it over and over, the easier it got until eventually it became second nature to me. Now I can hardly hit a nail with a hammer without a big kiap! I let it out in front of crowds (in my personal defense classes—not at the mall) all the time and it doesn't bother me a bit anymore. It is a great attention getter!

 Even though it's a simple thing, I know how hard it is to yell like this. That is why I say practice it! Don't think you'll just "yell" out of nowhere. You might scream, but that is not a ferocious battle cry. Don't worry, you'll still be making noise if you scream and that is good, but how much better prepared will you be for your own personal defense if you have a battle cry and are not afraid to use it! Your battle cry will make your "secret weapon" even more powerful! Practice it— give your family a thrill (or a scare)!

We are what we repeatedly do. Excellence then is not an act but a habit.

-Aristotle

Remember:
- A physical attack is not the end of the road, you still have choices.
- When adrenaline pumps, focus it into RAGE.
- RAGE – Righteous Anger Giving Energy – is not instinctive to everyone.
- Learn to RAGE by visualizing yourself as a ferocious animal.
- Use RAGE as your "secret weapon."
- Make a lot of noise. Practice your "battle cry" as you practice your "secret weapon."

Chapter Eight

Choose to Hit 'Em Where It Hurts

"Do something. If it works, do more of it.
If it doesn't, do something else."
—Attributed to Franklin D. Roosevelt

In this chapter:
- You Have Powerful Survival Instincts
- Take Immediate Action
- His Targets
- Your Weapons
- Ground Defense   • It Isn't Pretty
- Keep It Simple   • Keep Attacking

You Have Powerful Survival Instincts

Do you remember wrestling with someone bigger when you were a child? If they held your hands, you'd kick. If they held your feet, you'd claw. If they held your hands and feet, you'd wriggle, snarl, bite, spit, etc. The point is when you wrestled as a child against an older, stronger opponent, there were no holds barred. You became a fighting machine with only one goal in mind—escape! Those were your survival instincts kicking in, and you still have them.

You have the instincts; the question is, "Will you be able to tap into them?" The answer is "yes!" You definitely can!

Remind yourself: "I believe the Lord, I believe I am His daughter, I believe in myself, and I have a choice. My choice is not to allow anyone to demean or hurt me in any way!" Now, get in front of that mirror and take a look at the new you as you practice saying, "Get away from me" or "Leave me alone," or as you transform into your animal, feel its fury, and shout its battle cry. (If you just can't look in the mirror, practice in your mind—but the mirror will really help you visualize what you are capable of.)

I'm sure you've heard that "practice makes perfect." Your personal defense is one area that you don't want to be average in. You want to be good, you want to be great, you want to be able to tap into the survival instincts you already have. The more you practice this attitude in your mind, the more instinctive it will become. You will be able to stand up for yourself or transform into your ferocious animal instinctively.

It Happened

The bell rang early one morning. When Sara opened the front door, a short, slight, nice-looking young man smiled and said apologetically, "Excuse me ma'am, I'm sorry to bother you, but we're working on some power lines on your street and may have knocked something out. Could I please get into your basement to check your electricity?" **CHOICE?**

"That's all right, come in," Sara said. As she turned to lead him to the basement door, the man grabbed her around the neck and threw her onto the couch. **CHOICE?** For a moment Sara couldn't move. She described herself as being stunned and felt paralyzed as much from surprise as from fear, but when the guy began ripping at her clothes, a **RAGING** anger took over her.

Almost without thinking, Sara reached for a table lamp next to the couch and brought it crashing down on the man's head.

This didn't knock him out, it just dazed him but it gave her time to rush over and grab the lamp from the other end table. Her assailant scrambled to his feet and ran out of the house.

If you were to try to picture an ideal target for a rape, or a rape-resistor, it wouldn't be Sara. In her fifties with gray in her hair, she dresses conservatively and has a motherly or grand-motherly appearance.

Her comments were that she didn't even know she had that kind of **RAGE** inside of her. She didn't remember planning to fight back. She was just so furious, she had to do something!

ALERT Sara wasn't a trained martial artist. She had an even better asset: her will to survive. Because she refused to be a victim, her survival instincts kicked in. It was this will, this personal defense attitude, which transformed her from the stunned stage that held her paralyzed into the RAGE that gave her the power to take action. Using her instincts, she was able to make use of the weapons available to her.

Take Immediate Action

In the event you are attacked, you must take immediate action. Your assailant does not expect resistance. The fact that you have decided and trained yourself to take action will be quite a surprise to any would-be attacker. Your RAGE will take him completely off guard. Stage your resistance immediately. An assailant will assume that he is in control. He will expect his victim to be so afraid that she will submit to his demands easily, or that she will panic and will be easily controlled. Your immediate

> ᭡ The point of power is always in the present moment.᭡
>
> -Louise Hay

resistance either to refuse his demands, run, yell, or RAGE, will take him completely off guard. This will give you added time to get away or take control of the assault yourself.

His Targets

No matter how big or strong an assailant is, there are certain places on his body where you can hit him and make him hurt. You need to know exactly where to hit him to cause the most damage. All men (and women too, for that matter) have vulnerable areas on their bodies, and their strength cannot protect them from attacks to those areas. When you strike, strike smart and make it count. Strike his prime target areas.

Did you ever see the movie *The Three Ninjas*? If you did, you will probably remember the dummy the boys' grandfather made for them, so they could practice their strikes and kicks. The dummy had lights on it in specific target areas that would light up if the boys hit that target with a solid strike or kick. In this way, their grandfather taught them where to aim their strikes to do the most damage.

When you have to physically defend yourself, do not flail. It will do no good to beat on an assailant's chest or arms. Instead, focus all of your adrenaline and RAGE at the prime target areas on your assailant's body. They are:

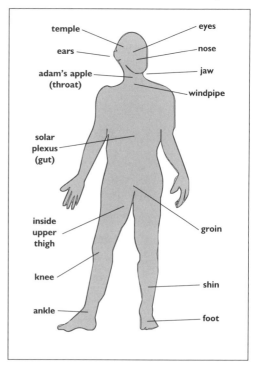

Knowing the areas of the body which, when hit, will cause the most pain and do the most damage will give your immediate resistance the upper edge. Deciding which target to hit is simply a matter of realizing what is exposed or available. The target areas are easy to memorize—go ahead and do that right now.

Notice how painful or weak those parts of your own body are if you push on them even just a little. Now think about how incapacitating it could be if they were struck with force from a fist, palm, elbow, or kick. An assailant cannot defend every part of his body at the same time. You must strike any exposed target immediately with whatever weapon you have available.

Your Weapons

Many parts of your body are very effective weapons if you choose to use them that way. By using the following weapons, your strike could either stun or distract your assailant momentarily, giving you enough time to get away, it could cause a painful distraction which would allow you to strike another target, or, as in the case of heavy strikes to the throat or windpipe, it could be fatal to your assailant. The following are some of your most effective weapons and some of the ways you can use them:

HEAD:

1) Action: Throw head back into assailant's nose, mouth, ears, jaw, or any part of his face.
   Effect: Break the nose or jaw, or crush bones in the face.

2) Action: Head butt into stomach.
   Effect: Knock the wind out of assailant.

MOUTH:

1) Action: Loudly screech into assailant's ear.
   Effect: Momentarily stun or distract him.

2) Action: Bite anything available—his fingers, nose, and genitals included. Bite with fury, to the bone, or tear the flesh.
   Effect: Painful distraction.

HANDS:

1) Action: Palm strike to nose or any target area.
   Effect: Break his nose or bones in his face, painful distraction, or stun him (depending on where you strike).

> **PALM STRIKE:** Using a fist for many females is awkward and often painful. A palm strike is a great option. Hold your hand up as if you were going to give a high-five. Instead of trying to slap the other person's hand with your full hand, lead out with your palm and hit their hand with your palm only. That is the motion. Now, to use it as a strike, use the same motion, with the force of your whole body behind it and aim for the nose!

2) Action: Fist strike to his throat or any target area.
   Effect: A strike to the throat by either a fist, palm, or knife hand, could cause gasping, choking, or even death. A fist into any other target area could cause a painful distraction or stun him momentarily.

3) Action: With fingers and thumbs close together and tight, slightly cup your hands, open your arms wide and quickly; with force, clap your cupped hands over an assailant's ears as if you were striking symbols in a band.
   Effect: A moderate blow will cause pain, a heavy blow might injure the inner ear.

KNIFE-HAND STRIKE: You've probably seen the knife-hand strike used by martial artists in action movies. To use a knife-hand, keep your hand stiff, fingers and thumb close together and tight. Now use the movement you would use if you were throwing a Frisbee with your hand held tight as described and aim for a target area: the throat, the side of the neck, the nose, etc.

4) Action: Claw—grab his testicles and ram them up into his pelvic bone.
   Effect: Extreme pain, momentary stunning.

5) Action: Yank his hair.
   Effect: Painful distraction.

FINGERS/THUMBS:

1) Action: Poke, claw, stab, or even gouge eyes with fingers or thumbs.
   Effect: Any attack to the eyes can cause serious injury or blindness. A stab to the eyes is a great way to get away from your assailant as quickly as possible. Often, the effect of losing his vision momentarily or possibly permanently will cause an assailant to stop his attack sooner than other strikes would. Stabbing or poking into an assailant's eyes with force could dislodge his eyeball.

2) Action: Keep fingers close together tightly and ram them into his windpipe.
   Effect: The effects of a blow to the windpipe range from gasping and choking to death.

ELBOWS:

1) Action: Thrust your elbows (like stabbing) in any direction: into his face, nose, ribs, solar plexus (gut), groin, or any vulnerable area.

   Effect: A hard, sharp blow to the ribs could break them. A blow to any other area has already been explained. Since your elbow is such a hard surface, it is an excellent weapon.

KNEES:

1) Action: Ram your knee into his groin. Anywhere you hit will hurt, but for the most damage, thrust your knee up under the groin, into his crotch, thereby crushing his genitals into his pelvic bone.

   Effect: Severe pain and stunning. If you hit him hard enough, you could render an assailant incapacitated for a brief time, or even unconscious if you strike with enough force.

2) Action: Ram your knee into his upper, inner thigh.

   Effect: Severe pain, and possibly numbing the leg if you strike with a great deal of force.

FEET:

1) Action: Kick any vulnerable area you can reach; specifically, the knees, shins, and foot. (Keep your kicks low or your assailant may be able to grab your leg.)

   Effect: Kicking to the knee, either side or front could either hyper-extend, dislocate the kneecap or, if hard enough, even break his leg. This target is one of my favorites. An assailant's natural reaction may be to guard his groin, but his knees are often available and one swift kick through one of them could make him unable to run.

2) Action: Scrape down shins with the edge of your shoe ending with a stomp on the foot or ankle.

   Effect: Scraping down his shins will cause a lot of pain. Stomping on his ankle or foot will not only cause a lot of pain, it could break either the ankle or small bones in his feet.

Don't limit yourself by thinking these are the only strikes possible. There are many ways to use your weapons against his targets. These suggestions are just a few of the possibilities. If you were being attacked, you would use whatever weapon you had available on whatever target was accessible in any way possible!

I doubt many of you have access to a gym with practice targets, or a masochistic friend who would allow you to practice using your weapons on him. However, you can still practice.

First, you can practice in your mind and in the air, wherever you are. (You could even use that mirror again.) Think about your weapons, study them, and practice throwing the strikes and kicks I have described. Second, ask a friend to hold up a pillow (off to the side) and practice striking it. Third, as you are watching TV or a movie, notice the dangerous situations people get themselves in and think about what you'd do, which weapon you'd use, and which target is accessible.

Any of these suggestions will help you get more comfortable with your

> It's funny, the more I practice the luckier I get.
> -Attributed to Arnold Palmer

weapons. The more practice you get, the greater your reflexes will be to throw that strike or kick if you ever have to.

Ground Defense

In doing research for his book, *Defend Yourself! Every Woman's Guide to Safeguarding Her Life,* Matt Thomas analyzed more than three thousand assaults against women. He found that in 40 percent of all such attacks, the victim was knocked to the ground before she knew what had happened (New York: Avon Books, 1995, p.19). Don't let this alarm you. Being on the ground may seem like a helpless position to be in, but in truth, staging your defense from the ground can actually be in your favor. Since most of a woman's strength is in her lower body, specifically in her legs, being on the ground will give you free use of the most powerful weapons you have. You can use these weapons in two ways:

First, as a shield: By keeping your legs between you and your assailant, you create a barrier to your torso that he will have a hard time getting through. I took a self defense class at Utah Valley State College and the instructor had us lie down on the ground, put our feet up, and try to keep him away from us. This proved to be very interesting to me. Though he tried hard, he was not able to get through my defenses. My legs were longer than his arms. Therefore, as he tried to reach out to me, he was stopped short. He was not able to harm me. As Mr. Thomas stated in his book, "Once you are on the ground, 99 percent of the time he (your assailant) will try to use his upper body against your lower body. Because you are in a defensive mode, he has to come to you. Since his arms are almost surely shorter than you legs, you now have the tactical advantage" (ibid). Therefore, being on the ground in this position is useful in your defense. However, you must keep your legs and feet between you and your attacker. That means you are turning, spinning, or rotating wherever necessary to keep yourself in this position (sort of like a break dance). You must not allow your assailant to get around your legs.

Second, as a position to launch your most powerful weapons: Those weapons are your legs, of course. In this position, an assailant will be trying to reach out for you, as I have described above. While he concentrates on finding a way to get to you, put up your legs as a shield and at the same time attack his vulnerable target areas. At some point in time, his knees or groin will become exposed. When they are, kick whatever is available! You would stay in this position, guarding yourself and finding an exposed area to kick, until you have landed a blow that stuns your assailant either momentarily or longer.

Once you feel confident that you can then get away, do so. However, do not get up from this position until you are sure your assailant is incapacitated. Continue your attack at any area that becomes exposed, using your legs as a shield and weapon. If your assailant falls to the ground, keep your legs between you and him, and continue your defense by throwing kicks at any target area you can reach until you feel you can get away safely.

It Happened

When Lisa's assailant knocked her to the floor, CHOICE? she didn't even try to get back up. Instead, she stayed where she was and kicked his groin with all of her strength. She had read that a woman's legs are four times stronger than her arms, so she put it to the test. She was grateful to find that her kick immobilized her attacker, giving her time to run out of the house and call for help.

 Once you are on the ground, do not try to get back up. You would have to stop your defense to do so and put yourself in a vulnerable position while you're attempting to stand. Defending from the ground is actually a very effective defense, use it!

It Isn't Pretty

Street fighting, or your personal defense, will not look like the staged fighting that you see on TV and in the movies. Actors always look so fluid and exact, every movement done with precision as if it was choreographed, which of course it was. Your personal defense against physical or sexual assault will be ugly. It will be survival! Remember, you must use whatever weapon you have available, on whatever target is accessible, in any way possible.

This means that if an assailant grabs you around the neck, you might bring your fist down hard into his groin and then continue your attack. If he grabs you in a bear hug from behind, you might throw your head back into his nose and then continue your attack. If his hands are around your throat, you might have to use your thumbs to gouge into his eyes and then continue your attack. If he tries to shove his genitals in your mouth, your only option may be to bite them as hard as you can and then continue your attack.

Thoughts of "gouging eyes" and "genital biting" are not pleasant ones, but I feel like I should bring them up because they are real possibilities. By bringing up some of the more lurid possibilities, I hope it will help you prepare yourself for anything. You must accept the fact that this kind of horrible thing is a possibility so that if any horrible thing ever happened to you, you could face it without being stunned into paralysis.

That means there could be blood, you could break your fingers when you strike, he will likely hurt you during your attack on him, and you could even be shot or stabbed. Personal defense means that until you can no longer move, you keep attacking!

Keep It Simple

The high-low defense is the easiest way to remember simple and effective personal defense. Simply stated, this means: if your assailant is guarding his lower body (usually the groin), attack high (nose, face, etc.). If your assailant's upper body/head is not accessible, attack low (knee, groin, etc). Your assailant cannot effectively guard both areas of his body at the same time, so go for the less-guarded area. As your attacker's focus is drawn to pain in the high area (perhaps while he covers his nose that you have just smashed your palm into), you would then strike his groin, knee, shin, ankle, or foot. As his focus is now directed to pain in the low area (while he stoops over from a blow to his groin), you would then ram your knee or palm into his nose. You would continue this high-low attack for as long as you felt you were in danger.

> In the middle of difficulty lies opportunity.
> –Attributed to Albert Einstein

Keep Attacking

During an attack, your goal is to get away. Don't expect a hard, well-aimed kick in the knee to stop your attacker, though it is a possibility. The truth is, you may be in it for the long haul. You must keep hitting, kicking, biting, twisting, or gouging until your attacker either takes off, becomes unconscious, or can no longer chase after you.

It Happened

Linda lived with her ex-father-in-law, he on one side of the house and she on the other. Though Linda was always careful to keep the doors locked, her father-in-law wasn't. One night, she came home from a date and heard footsteps in the hall.

CHOICE? Knowing her ex-father-in-law and son were asleep, she went out of her room to investigate. Suddenly, a man jumped her, grabbed her by the throat, and pinned her against the wall. CHOICE? Instantly, she flew into a RAGE, more out of anger than fear. The first thing she did was stomp on his foot. She then kneed him in the groin, bit his neck, punched him in the gut (solar plexus), smashed her palm into his nose, clawed him with her fingers, and hit him with a lamp. Soon, she had him nailed against the door, which he gratefully opened and took off.

During the attack, Linda herself suffered pain as the assailant grabbed her neck and wrists. Despite this pain, however, she continued her RAGING attack on her assailant until her life was no longer in jeopardy.

Remember:
- You have powerful survival instincts. Tap into them by visualizing and practicing your personal defense attitude.
- Get in front of the mirror and practice your RAGE. The more you practice this attitude, the more instinctive it will become.
- Your assailant does not expect resistance. Take immediate action.
- Learn to strike the prime target areas of the body.
- Recognize the weapons you have on your own body. Visualize and practice using them.
- Staging your defense from the ground can actually be in your favor. Use your legs as a shield and a weapon.
- Street fighting isn't pretty, it is survival.
- You must use whatever weapon you have available, on whatever target is available, in any way possible.
- Keep it simple. Use the high-low defense.
- Keep attacking until you can get away.

Choose to Hit and Hit Hard

"Do or do not. There is no try."
—Yoda

In this chapter:
- Use Appropriate Resistance
- Strike All the Way Through
- Strike Over and Over and Over
- It Is More Important to Be Committed Than Trained

Use Appropriate Resistance

Every situation is different. You would not send a throat-crushing blow into someone's windpipe because he put his hand on your leg. Verbal resistance, or possibly an elbow into the gut (solar plexus), or even a pinch to the inside of the thigh should send your assailant on his way. However, if your attacker threatens you with bodily harm and his throat is an available target, you would then be justified in sending him a crushing blow. Any blow to the throat or windpipe could be fatal, so you must use caution with this defense.

Don't worry about doing or not doing the "right" thing if you are being assaulted. Often when I teach a class, seminar, or fireside, people will talk to me afterward. As they tell me their experiences, over and over I will hear statements such as "I don't know why I said . . . but it stopped him from . . ." or "I don't know how I knew to hit him there" or "I just felt like I shouldn't be with him, so I left." Remember, the Spirit can be with you and He will lead and guide you. With the knowledge you are gaining of assailants, their patterns, and what your choices are, the Spirit will be able to bring to your mind the appropriate response to any situation you may be faced with. Just be sure to keep your buddy with you and act on His promptings. He's your best friend and greatest personal defense tool you will ever have!

Strike All the Way Through

In Tae Kwon Do, we break boards. There are at least two reasons for this that I know of. The first is to demonstrate that we know the technique involved. The second is to learn to strike or kick all the way through the board, thus using our full power.

If we strike the board, the chances of it breaking are next to none. If we visualize and strike through the board, it will break. The difference is that subconsciously, unless we visualize going all the way through the board, we actually stop our strike at the board or "pull our punch," which does not break it. Even though we feel like we're hitting it our hardest, we just aren't. However, if we concentrate on striking through the board, our hands or feet fly through it almost as if it wasn't there. It's a pretty awesome feeling!

I have broken five boards at a time with a back-side kick. It didn't feel any harder to me than breaking one or two boards. If you visualize your kicks and strikes going all the way through your assailant's knee, groin, nose, foot, or jaw, imagine the impact your blows will carry with them! If I can go through five boards, you can go through a knee like butter!

Strike Over and Over and Over

Often, an assailant will be high on something. He may be drunk, stoned, or doped up. In this condition, the phrase "feeling no pain" applies, which basically means that he will not feel the pain as quickly as someone else would. In this "numb" state, it will take more strikes and more pain to affect him than it would for someone not on these drugs.

Even though it may take a lot of effort on your part, through your RAGE and commitment to survival, he will eventually "feel the pain." However, you must mentally prepare yourself to realize that you are not Superwoman; one blow from you will not necessarily save the day. You must continue striking until he is incapacitated. This could be one strike, two strikes, or thirty strikes. Don't ever give up! Keep striking even if you're feeling pain yourself. Never stop your defense until you can get away.

It Is More Important to Be Committed Than Trained

The reason I selected most of the stories I have throughout this book is because they represent everyday, "real life" untrained women. None of the women I've mentioned in this book have had formal personal defense training (except me), but the successful ones have all had a will to survive. Their stories are inspiring and insightful.

In fact, I believe that a burning RAGE and a commitment to survival are more effective than any kind of formal training you could have. I have heard a story about a female black-belt in Tae Kwon Do who was shamed by her instructor because she was not able to stop an attack on herself. Though she had been trained physically, she did not have a personal defense attitude that included a commitment to survive.

The more you learn, the more confident you will become; the more confident you become, the less likely you are to ever be a victim in the first place; and if you were to be assaulted, the more likely you would be to thwart an attack. That is why I spend so much time in this book teaching you the attitude. By combining a will to survive with a little knowledge of defense tactics, you will have a powerful combination.

It Happened

While sitting on a bench in a park used frequently by joggers, Jill was attacked by a vicious assailant. Tackling her from behind, the two tumbled down the side of a small hill. As they rolled to the bottom of the hill, Jill's face was slammed into the mud. The man, kneeling on her neck and shoulders, pushed her face into the ground, and began choking her. CHOICE? Realizing that she would not last long, she purposely went limp.

As she went limp, her assailant gained confidence in his efforts and turned her over onto her back. Jill was terrified as she caught sight of her attacker. With a nylon pulled over his head, he looked frightening. CHOICE? Instantly, she began screaming as loud as she could. Caught off guard, her assailant ordered her to "shut up!" CHOICE? This made her scream even louder. He seemed to be shocked at the resistance of this crazy screaming woman.

Suddenly, he pulled out a knife which ENRAGED her. CHOICE? Acting on pure adrenaline, she reached out and grabbed the knife. She wrapped her hand tightly around the jagged blade and blood was everywhere. She said that at this point, "she became the aggressor." As he put his hand over her mouth to shut her up, one of his fingers fell slightly into her mouth. She thought to herself, "You're going to pay for this!" and bit through to the bone. Her attacker pulled back in agony, got up, and ran.

I've often told people that if I could just have 5 seconds to tell them the most important things they should know about their own personal defense, I would say: Listen to the Spirit, learn to RAGE, and commit to survive. I suppose that would have made a pretty short book. However, unless you understand what those things mean, I don't suppose you could really use them very effectively!

Remember:

- Every situation is different. Use appropriate resistance for the situation you are in.
- To use as much force as you are capable of, strike all the way through your target.
- You must continue to strike over and over and over until you can get away.
- It is more important to be committed to your own survival than to be trained in fighting skills.
- By combining a will to survive with a little knowledge of defense tactics, you will have a powerful combination!

Choose to Make Choices While You Still Have Them

"Opportunities are multiplied as they are seized."
—Sun Tzu

In this chapter:
• There Are No Guarantees
• To Resist or Not to Resist
• Crime Scene One Will Always Be Better Than Crime Scene Two

There Are No Guarantees

No matter how aggressive your personal defense is, you could still be killed, especially if your assailant has a weapon. I've already told you the way I feel about the choices I've made for myself concerning my own personal defense. Now you have to make your own choices by weighing the consequences of resistance versus non-resistance. The fact is, you need to weigh those choices now and make your decisions now. (Have I made that clear yet?) Don't wait until you are in a dangerous situation to decide how you will react, and don't assume that you will make the choice to resist naturally; many of us don't.

The one guarantee that you do have is that if you are assaulted and you do not resist, your assailant will have total control over you and your situation. You will have to submit to his demands, whatever they may be (unless, of course, some super hero comes to your rescue—fat chance).

To Resist or Not to Resist

Resisting immediately is my personal choice. Resist while you still have choices, even if your assailant has a weapon and threatens to kill you. The harsh reality is that resisting may get you killed on the spot. That would still be your choice—not his. If his intentions were to shoot you immediately, he would have done so already. If he threatens you with a weapon and demands that you go with him, his intentions may still be to use his weapon on you, but he has other plans for you first. It's those "other plans" that I refuse to go along with. If you do not take a stand and choose your own fate, every step you take in compliance with your attacker reduces your choices, until eventually you have none.

This is when knowing you are a daughter of God and having a healthy awareness of death and its part in

> If you limit your choices only to what seems possible or reasonable, you disconnect yourself from what you truly want, all that is left is a compromise.
> -Robert Fritz

your progression will help you. Though you may think it is scary to think of dying, in reality, death is a new beginning. This knowledge will help you put aside your fears in the face of possible death, and will make you strong and able to RAGE. You might think to yourself, "You may send me out of this life, but I'll be taking a piece of you with me!" The interesting thing about this attitude is that just the fact that you put up resistance will likely stop the attack, but if not, your RAGE will give you a fighting chance to survive.

Crime Scene One Will Always Be Better Than Crime Scene Two

To illustrate this point, consider the following scenario:

You are walking down the street and an assailant comes toward you. He threatens you with a gun and demands that you go into the alley with him. What are some of your choices?

1) Resist immediately by running away from him (in a curved line, to a place of safety).
2) Resist immediately through RAGE. Kick through your assailant's knee and continue striking at his exposed target areas, making a lot of noise and drawing the attention of other people to your situation.
3) Go with him.

You choose to go with him into the alley. He now grabs hold of you and throws you to the ground. What are your choices?

1) In the quiet and secluded alley, resist from the ground, defend yourself by RAGING. Kick through your assailant's knee and continue to strike his target areas.
2) Lie there.

You choose to lie there, waiting for what he will do next. He now binds your hands and feet with tight cords and gags you. What are your choices?

0) You have none.

You are now at his disposal to do with as he pleases. That could involve torture, rape, or possibly murder. Do you see how your choices get fewer and fewer with each step you take in submission to your assailant's demands?

Stage your defense on your terms. Do not allow yourself to be taken to another location, which would be on your assailant's "turf." Every scenario will be different, and every outcome will be unique, but one thing is for sure: Your choices will diminish with each step you take in compliance with your assailant until eventually you will have no more choices, and that is the scariest of all positions to be in.

Remember:
- No matter how aggressive your personal defense is, you could still be injured or even killed.
- If you do not take a stand and choose your own fate, every step you take in compliance with your attacker reduces your choices, until eventually you have none.
- My choice is to resist immediately, even if my assailant has a weapon. You must make your own choice.
- Crime Scene One will always be better than Crime Scene Two.
- To be under the total control of an assailant is the scariest of all places to be in.

Chapter Eleven

Choose Not to Fall Prey to Date Rape

"If passion drives you, let wisdom hold the reins."
—Benjamin Franklin

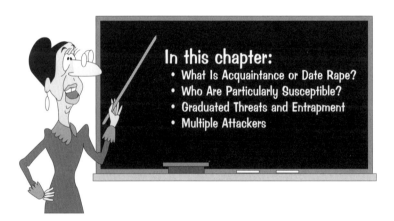

In this chapter:
• What Is Acquaintance or Date Rape?
• Who Are Particularly Susceptible?
• Graduated Threats and Entrapment
• Multiple Attackers

What Is Acquaintance or Date Rape?

Acquaintance rape accounts for most of all rape incidents. In a study of 3,187 female students from college campuses conducted by Mary Koss[1], one in four women surveyed was a victim of rape or

---

[1] Koss, M.P. & Dinero, T.E. (1988). A discriminate analysis of risk factors among a national sample of college women. *Journal of Consulting and Clinical Psychology*, 57, 133-147 as found in David G. Curtis, Ph.D., B.C.E.T.S., "Perspectives on Acquaintance Rape," *Clinical Psychologist*, (1997).

attempted rape. Of those, 84 percent knew their attackers, and 57
percent of those rapes happened
while on dates.

> **DATE RAPE:** Specifically, a rape perpetrated by someone the victim is dating. It could be some-one she knows only casually and has just begun dating, or it might be someone she has an even longer relationship with, such as her boyfriend.

Look at these statistics and
realize what they are telling you.
It is important to be cautious and
alert to assaults that could come
from a stranger. However, the fact is, most rapes are actually carried
out by someone whom the victim knows, either casually, such as an
acquaintance, or in a more intimate relationship such as dating. The
sobering reality is that you
are more likely to be sexually assaulted on a date,
at a party, at a friend's
house, or even in your
own home by someone
you know than you are to
be targeted by a stranger.

> **ACQUAINTANCE RAPE:** Rape per-petrated by someone known to the victim. It could be a friend, neighbor, or co-work-er; someone she has a casual relationship with. In statistics, "date rape" is included as an acquaintance rape since the victim knows her assailant in both cases.
> A graphic definition would include: being subjected to unwanted intercourse, oral sex, anal sex, or any other sexual contact through the use of menacing verbal pres-sure, misuse of authority, force, or threat of force.

Another sobering sta-
tistic is found in a study
which states that 60% of
the college-aged men
interviewed said they would commit rape if they knew they could
get away with it [2], and that was way back in the late 1980's! Certainly
we can assume that attitudes towards women are not getting more
respectful, quite the opposite. Society is taking a downward spiral
in its views on respect, sex, and appropriate relationships. As long
as women are portrayed as objects, and sexual desire and power is
pounded into us, especially through the media, attitudes towards
women will get progressively worse.

---

[2] Valerie Frankel, "Why Rape Statistics Don't Add Up," *Mademoiselle Magazine*, December 1991 as found in Judith Fein, Ph.D., *Exploding the Myth of Self-Defense*, Duncans Mills, California: Torrance Publishing, pp. 81.

Who Are Particularly Susceptible?

Teenagers and young single working women are particularly susceptible to acquaintance or date rape. There are a few possible reasons for this: it may be because they are naive, or because they socialize more, attend more parties, meet more people, have a larger circle of friends, or maybe they are just more trusting. Whatever the reason, the bottom line is that they ignore the same warning signals which would warn them of a stranger's intentions simply because they know their "friend" or "date," and therefore their guard is down.

A young woman could be flattered to be asked out. It is common to find a young woman dating someone whom she is not totally comfortable with simply because he is paying attention to her or because he is a "really nice guy most of the time." She might ignore her feelings of discomfort, thinking that she knows the guy she is with so it will be okay. She could be lured into a compromising situation just because she blindly trusts someone she thinks she knows.

It Happened

A fourteen-year-old girl and her boyfriend were supposed to be attending early morning seminary at their church. Her boyfriend talked her into skipping the class and going into another classroom. CHOICE? Sometime during their time together, in which they were "making out," he ended up raping her. CHOICE?

The young woman was too ashamed to have been skipping seminary with him in the church classroom in the first place to tell anyone except a few friends about the incident. She also did not think anyone would believe her; it was her word against his that the act wasn't consensual.

Graduated Threats and Entrapment

If you are dating someone who makes you feel uncomfortable in any way, stop dating him. Listen to the Spirit and avoid a dangerous situation by simply getting out of it. Unfortunately, many women either do not trust their own feelings or their desire to be liked overrides their feelings of caution.

Just about anyone who has gone through the horror of an acquaintance or date rape will tell you that they were tipped off by their feelings but they ignored them. They will say things like, "I knew I shouldn't go out with him," or "he had been making me uneasy all night."

This is an awkward situation. He isn't letting you off the hook.

It Could Happen

You're at a party with a young man that you have known and liked for three weeks. This particular night he is acting a little different, saying things to you that are just on the edge of being inappropriate. CHOICE? You are a little uncomfortable but laugh it off, thinking he is just acting silly. As the night goes on, his hands begin wandering and touching you inappropriately, which makes you very uncomfortable. CHOICE? You begin to think that you really should go home, and you wonder how you can make excuses that won't seem stupid or make you look uptight. CHOICE? You tell him that you really aren't feeling very well and you don't want him to have to leave the party, so you'll just call your parents and ask them to pick you up and take you home. He tells you that he won't hear of it and that he wants to take you home himself. By this time, you really do not want to be alone with him. CHOICE?

You are feeling that you want to leave, and you really don't want to be alone with him, but he's being a "gentleman" and offering to take you. Now you either have to say, "No, I'm not comfortable going home with you," or you have to let him take you home.

What would happen if you let him take you home? Perhaps nothing. You don't really know how this or any situation will actually end up, but remember the discomfort you have been feeling? Where is that coming from? Is it your imagination or is the Spirit trying to tell you something?

Your personal alarm system is going off, don't ignore it. Your buddy is trying to steer you clear of upcoming danger. The Spirit is warning you, but it's up to you to "hearken" (which means listen and obey) to that still small voice.

The only thing that would stop you from following through and calling your parents to come and get you or asking another friend to take you home is embarrassment. You would feel so stupid. He hasn't hurt you, and he is offering to take you home, so you would insult him and look like you were really over-reacting if you refused to let him.

ALERT This is a common date rape scenario. The details may be different but the graduated threat and the uncomfortable feelings have been felt by many women who have experienced this kind of scenario. If you allow him to take you home, you have now put yourself into a situation which is called "entrapment."

Your date has now manipulated you into being alone with him (trapped). By allowing yourself to be alone with him, even though you are uncomfortable, you have failed his test and shown him that you can be controlled. Now that he has you all to himself, it is only your word against his that this "rape" was not consensual sex between a boyfriend and girl-friend. He's confident you will never tell, and usually, a girl in this situation never does.

If you were in this situation and your date's behavior became inappropriate in any way, do not laugh or shrug it off thinking it's no big deal. It is a big deal. He is demonstrating a lack of respect for you that is demeaning and could be dangerous. Look

him in the eyes, tell him to "Cut it out," and make it perfectly clear through your attitude and body language that you will not allow him to treat you that way. This should handle the situation, however, if you continue to feel uncomfortable around him, get away from him! No apologies, no excuses. Make it clear that you will not be with him and get a ride home.

You cannot tell by the way he looks if your acquaintance could turn into an assailant any more than you can spot a stranger who would assault you. You also cannot tell by the way he acts much of the time. If your friend or date is trying to manipulate you, he will generally be quite pleasant and attentive at first. However, there are a few attitudes and behaviors that can "tip you off" to the fact that he could have a high level of hostility and may potentially be volatile or dangerous.

1) Emotional intimidation:
   Belittling comments
   Ignoring
   Sulking

2) Coercive tendencies:
   Dictating friends or dress
   Projecting an air of superiority
   Acting like he knows you much better than he actually does

3) Physical Intimidation:
   Body posturing (such as blocking a doorway)
   Getting pleasure from physically startling or scaring you

4) Harboring negative feelings about women in general:
    Speaking of previous girlfriends with ridicule or scorn

5) Potentially volatile:
    Extreme jealousy
    Inability to handle emotional frustration without anger

6) Taking offense if you do not want to go to activities
    which could limit your resistance such as:
    Drinking alcohol
    Going to a private or isolated place

 If you see any of these signs of potential aggression or
ALERT volatility in your "friend," you owe it to yourself, as a daughter of God, to get out of the situation or relationship. His hostility towards you or other women at the very least could harm you emotionally, and the likelihood of him becoming physically dangerous is high. It is also very possible that the Spirit will alert you to potential problems even before you see any "signs." I'll say it again, if you feel uncomfortable for any reason, or no reason at all, get yourself out of the situation you are in immediately.

Multiple Attackers

Teenagers often become the victims of more than one attacker. This happens sometimes during social occasions, such as at a friend's house or at a party. Often, a young woman will get herself into a situation that is beyond her control. She may be drinking or tricked into drinking alcohol, and she may have even had a relationship with one of the "team," or "fraternity," or group of friends. (Remember, any time there is alcohol or drugs involved, your chances of becoming a victim rise substantially.) The gang mentality is heightened with substance abuse, and any female finding herself accessible to this group of assailants could become their easy victim. Typically she is separated from her friends and led into an isolated area where she is alone with this "group." There she will be raped by any or all of the group, or "gang-raped."

It Happened

Tara, seventeen, went with her boyfriend to one of his friend's homes. The night was spent "partying" and Tara, as well as others, consumed alcohol. Eventually, she went into the bedroom with her boyfriend, and as she did, a few of his friends followed, wanting to have group sex with her. When she objected, she was gang-raped by four teenage boys.

The mentality of a "gang rape" is all about male bonding. Oblivious to a young woman's pleas or cries, they take turns sexually assaulting her and cheering each other on. Dr. Fein explains, "No one tries to stop the rape. The men believe the woman "asked for it" or "deserved it," and they have no guilt or remorse. They don't feel they raped their victim, whom they consider a "slut" or "tramp." They maintain their code of silence and are supportive of teammates."[3] (or friends)

 Be as alert with an acquaintance as you would be with a stranger. Acquaintance or date rape falls into the assault pattern perfectly, and you can stop this assault the same way you would stop a stranger. Don't be fooled by the fact that you know him. If he crosses over your line of comfort in any way, he has just become a stranger to you!

[3] Judith Fein, Ph.D., *Exploding the Myth of Self-Defense*, Duncans Mills, California: Torrance Publishing, pp.83-84.

Listen to the Spirit! Follow the warning feelings you get despite your fear of embarrassment. Stop the date any time your personal alarm goes off. (That could be even before it starts.) Trust the Spirit and trust yourself.

Remember:

- Most rapes are actually carried out by someone the victim knows.
- Teenagers and young single working women are particularly susceptible to date rape.
- Your feelings will often tip you off, don't ignore them!
- In an acquaintance or date rape scenario, an assailant will typically manipulate his victim into being alone with him. There it will be his word against hers that the sex wasn't consensual.
- Teenagers are often the victims of more than one attacker at a time.
- Choose to date only young men that you feel totally comfortable with.
- Choose to end any date or relationship that begins to make you uncomfortable.
- Be as alert with an acquaintance as you would be around strangers. Don't ignore the Spirit just because you think you know someone.

Chapter Twelve

Choose to Use Car Safety

"Every one thinks of changing the world,
but no one thinks of changing himself."
—Leo Tolstoy

In this chapter:
- The Safest Way to Travel
- Carjacking
- If You Are Followed in Your Car
- More About Car Safety
- Just a Few More Tips

The Safest Way to Travel

The safest way to travel in your car is to lock your doors, keep your windows rolled up, and keep your music down. As long as you are in your car with the doors locked, you are relatively safe. If you leave your car or do not lock your doors, you open up all kinds of opportunities for assault. I have heard story after story of women brutalized and murdered simply because their attackers jumped into their cars while they were at a stop sign, a stoplight, or inching forward in heavy traffic.

It Happened

My mother told me a story that happened to her many years ago that "opened her eyes" to the ease with which someone can enter your car if your doors are not locked. She was stopped at a light driving from Provo to Orem, Utah when a little woman jerked open the passenger door and jumped into her car. "How about taking me home?" the woman asked (assuming the answer would be yes since she was already in the car). My mom was stunned. She asked the woman why in the world she would just jump into someone's car like that and the woman responded that she always traveled that way. Mom took her home and vowed to never leave her car doors unlocked again.

Luckily, mom's incident was almost comical. Many women are not so fortunate. Their intruders have sinister intentions which often include rape and murder.

An assailant can have access into your car through your car window also. Though it feels great to drive with your windows down on a beautiful day, you should never leave your windows down more than a few inches. If your windows are all the way down, an assailant can reach into your car and grab your purse (keep it off the seat and out of reach). He can also reach in and assault you.

It Happened

Trina was driving home from her Tae Kwon Do class one night. She had her windows rolled down, and while stopped at a stop sign, a drunk leaned in through the passenger window and tried to fondle her breasts. CHOICE? She had the presence of mind to throw a back-fist into his face and he painfully dislodged himself from her window and staggered off.

Now what about that radio? I've been stopped at a stoplight in my car and had someone stop behind me whose car radio was on so loud that it actually rocked my car a little, even with my windows rolled up. I'll bet you've had the same experience: either you're me, or you're the car behind me, right? I'm not going to go so far as to tell you that playing your music loudly is dangerous. However, playing your music too loud puts you at a disadvantage. You will lose your sense of "hearing things around you." You might not be as alert to any dangers or situations you may encounter on the road. It wouldn't hurt to turn it down a little.

Carjacking

Drive an ugly car (just kidding). If someone wants your car, let him have it! If he wants you also, that is a different story. Your car isn't worth risking your life. However, carjackers will often take the driver with them or force them into the trunk. Many situations like this end up with the death of the driver.

It Happened

One Fall morning, an armed man ordered Jamie out of her car as she was stopped at a red light. CHOICE? Instead of submitting to his demands, she stepped on the gas and sped through the intersection. A mile up the road she stopped to call the police, but there was no sign of the gunman by the time the officers arrived.

What can you do? First of all, notice who and what is around you while stopped at a stoplight, stop sign, or in traffic. Be alert when exiting or approaching your car. Don't get out or continue to approach your car if you feel uncomfortable. Also, make it a habit to lock your doors and check your back seat before entering your car. Second, if somehow an assailant would happen to get into your car and order you to "drive," do not hesitate to stage your resistance. Do this by crashing into a pole, sidewalk, or building, anything that will call attention to yourself right away, while you are still in familiar territory and going slow. Don't wait to reach high speeds or to have traveled into a secluded area to stage your resistance.

If an assailant threatens you with a weapon and demands that you get into your trunk, what do you do? There is no way on earth I would get into my trunk; I would stage my resistance right then and there. Once I was in that trunk, my choices would be way too limited. Here comes my RAGE!

If You Are Followed in Your Car

This can happen to anyone. An assailant may notice you while driving or he may notice you walking to your car and follow you to your home. Once again, you must be alert. Pay attention to the cars driving behind you.

It Happened

I was working as a telephone operator through the evening, getting off work around 11:00 p.m. The office I was working at was about 20 minutes from my home. One night as I drove home, I noticed a car with only one headlight behind me. Because it was quite a long way home and there were many twists and turns in my route, the fact that this car was still behind me after about 15 minutes began to alarm me. **CHOICE?** I would probably have done it differently today, knowing what I know now, but at that time in my life I wasn't overly safety-conscious nor did I have a clue what to do. Thank heavens the Spirit guided me that night.

Knowing that my subdivision was coming up soon and I was about one eighth of a mile ahead of this car, I turned into my subdivision, quickly turned down the first street and into the first driveway, and turned out my lights. I then saw this car turn into my subdivision and continue down the street. My heart was racing. I stayed there for about ten minutes before I felt okay about continuing home.

ALERT You do not want to bring trouble home with you. You must be alert and notice who is behind you. The rule of thumb is three turns: if you feel like someone could be following you, make three turns. If he is still with you, you may want to make a couple more. If the car seems to be following you, do not go home! Proceed to a well-lit public place and call for help, or drive right to a police or fire station and lay on your horn. Do anything you have to do to avoid bringing a predator home with you or ending up in a secluded place with him.

More About Car Safety

Driving a car is a big responsibility. You probably learned "defensive driving" in your Driver's Education classes. Let's just add a few more "defensive" tips that will aid you in your own personal safety while you are operating or riding in a car.

- Lock your car doors while you are getting gas.
- Park in well-lit areas.
- If your car breaks down where you feel it's too risky to get out, stay inside with your flashers on, doors locked, windows rolled up tight, and wait for the police. (Having a cell phone with you is a great personal defense tool.) If someone stops to help, talk through the glass or roll the window down only a couple of inches. Ask them to call for help. Accept no other offers.
- Don't stop at the scene of a breakdown. Drive to the nearest phone to summon help.

- Beware of another driver who signals that you have a flat tire or other problem. This is a common ruse for getting an intended victim stopped. It's safest to slow down but keep going, even if you ruin a tire rim. (I've done that.) If you do stop, leave your engine running. Don't get out until you're sure no one has pulled up behind you.

It Happened

My sister and I were driving along the freeway from Florida to Georgia to see my mother when a man in the car behind us pulled up along the side of our car and motioned that something was wrong with our van. So there we were, not knowing if he was telling the truth, but also not wanting to ignore a warning from a well-meaning person that would be helpful to us. **CHOICE?**

We pulled off the side of the freeway and stayed in the van as the man approached our window. I rolled the window down about two inches and he told us that our back tire was wobbling and he was afraid it might loosen up enough to fall off. We felt comfortable that he was telling us the truth. He didn't pressure us to get out or do anything which would alert us to danger. **CHOICE?** We thanked him and took a look at the tire ourselves as the man drove off. He was right. The tire was in terrible shape and we were lucky enough to be close to an exit which we slowly drove off with our blinkers flashing, and found the help we needed to get the van fixed.

ALERT I tell you this simple story of a good Samaritan because most of the time if someone is trying to tell you something about your car, it will be true. However, you have to use caution, because it could also be a ploy. Stay in your car and thank your "protector." You will then have to make decisions about what to do next depending on your situation. Use common sense and let the Spirit guide your decisions.

Just a Few More Tips

So where do all these "safety tips" come from anyway? I'm sure you realize that someone isn't sitting around making them up. They come from the experiences of others. Through their experiences, we can learn how to help ourselves.

The reason I bring this up is because sometimes you may hear a tip and think, "Okay, that's a good idea," or "I don't need to worry about that," and go along your merry way without ever thinking about it again. Please don't do that. Read the tips and use them. Someone else had to learn them the hard way. Don't let that happen to you!

- If you are walking down a street and are harassed from a vehicle, turn and walk in the opposite direction or cross the street.
- When possible, walk facing traffic in the middle of the sidewalk away from parked cars, doorways, bushes, or alleys.
- Don't leave your house keys on your key chain when giving them to a repairman, valet, etc. Give only the car key.
- Do not meet with photographers, modeling agents, etc. in private, secluded, out-of-the-way locations. Be very suspicious if anyone refuses to meet with you in an established, occupied office during normal working hours. Always take someone along with you.
- If responding to a "help wanted" or "classified ad," never meet in a quiet, secluded place. Take someone along with you, and if you feel uncomfortable for any reason, leave.
- Set up a family "password." This word would be used in an emergency situation when someone who is unfamiliar to another family member is asked to deliver an important message to him or her. It will allow the family member to know that the message being given is real.

How lucky for that young girl that her family had talked about

It Happened

Cindy, age 11, was walking down the street when a man stopped and told her to hurry and get into his car. He said that her mom was in the hospital and he was supposed to take her there. **CHOICE?** Cindy, not knowing the man, asked, "What's the password?" He stammered a bit and said, "Uh, candy?" She said, "No!" Then she screamed and ran away from him.

what to do if this situation ever happened to them. Don't put off your own preparation, make your decisions and do it now!

There are many other safety tips I could list. Most of them are common sense so I'll sum it up with this: Listen to the Spirit and use common sense! Use common sense that you already have, and things you have learned from reading this book. Accept the fact that even though most people are wonderful, there are a few that would hurt you—maybe even in your own neighborhood. It's those few that you have to watch out for and take precautions against so that they do not hurt you.

Remember:

• The safest way to travel in your car is with the doors locked, the windows rolled up, and the music turned down.
• If someone wants your car, let him have it. Your car is not worth risking your life.
• Be prepared to "crash" your car into something, if necessary, to interrupt an assault.
• Do not bring trouble home with you. Be aware of who and what is around you as you are driving. If you notice that a car seems to be following you, drive to a public place or police station.
• Listen to the Spirit and use common sense. Follow every safety tip you possibly can.

Chapter Thirteen

Choose to Watch and Pray Always

"Knowledge becomes power only when we put it to use."
—Unknown

In this chapter:
• One Last Safety Tip

One Last Safety Tip

"Watch and pray always . . ." (3 Nephi 18:15). The Lord loves you and is deeply concerned for your welfare. His counsel to "watch and pray always . . ." suggests that we pray every day for His protection and then we watch—watch ourselves that we use wisdom and caution, and watch to see His hand as He guides and protects us.

It Happened

A few weeks before Rebecca was to visit the Atlanta Georgia Temple, she began having nightmares of a man robbing her, getting away with her purse, credit cards, checks, and driver's license.

The day before her trip to the temple, her concern became so great that she checked her wallet over and over to make sure everything was there, including her temple recommend. That evening, arriving at a party held at the church, she once again checked to make sure her wallet, lipstick, and mirror were in her purse. She felt comforted and secure knowing that she had asked for the Lord's protection.

As she approached the church, she felt someone behind her. Turning around, she was faced with an assailant who demanded that she give him her purse as he began tugging at her arm. While she struggled to free herself from her attacker, her purse flew across the lawn and landed in the bushes. Her assailant ran off, grabbing her purse as he left.

Distressed at the loss of her purse, Rebecca called the police and then found a quiet place in the church where she tearfully prayed to her Father in Heaven, telling him that she couldn't understand why this had happened to her when she had prayed for His protection. Now her wallet was gone, with everything in it, including her temple recommend—she wouldn't even be able to go to the temple the next day as she had planned.

The police officers, combing the area, found neither her purse nor her assailant. Feeling helpless and hopeless, Rebecca walked to her car. As she walked, she felt an impression to go look in the grass again to see if anything had fallen out of her purse. Searching, she found her keys reflecting in the moonlight. Happily, she started back towards her car and felt like she ought to check the bushes also. Much to her relief and joy, she found her wallet with everything, including her temple recommend, intact. Dumbfounded, one of the police officers told her, "I've never seen someone so lucky." Rebecca was quick to correct him, remarking, "It's protection from God." Joking, she added, "The guy did get one thing of value though—my lipstick!" When no one laughed, Rebecca looked to see what was causing their silence. There, by the bushes, was her lipstick sitting upright on the little mirror which had been in her purse. (Rebecca Thomas, *Ensign*, June 2003, pp. 70, 71)

What a wonderful blessing it is to know that your Father in Heaven is watching over you. You know that not every story turns out "happily" like Rebecca's did. Bad things can still happen to good people who have asked the Lord for protection. His ways are not our ways, and part of our mortal experience will include pain and sorrow. However, He will give us specific blessings which include watching over our safety when it is within His purposes for us, if we ask Him.

Don't take for granted or turn your back on the precious protection that your Father offers you. Pray to Him always and ask Him to guide and protect you. With His help, you can face up to the realities of mortality and ". . . Be of good cheer . . ." (Acts 27:25), you are never alone. Remember, the Lord has promised you, ". . . I will go before your face. I will be on your right hand and on your left, and my Spirit shall be in your hearts, and mine angels round about you, to bear you up" (D&C 84:88).

Chapter Fourteen

Now Let's Practice

"It is the ability to choose which makes us human."
—Madeleine L'Engle

In this chapter:

- What Would You Do?
- In Conclusion

I hope you have made some decisions about your own personal defense by now. Just to give you some practice using the decisions you've made, I'm going to give you some true, real-life scenarios to think about, which really happened, and which could happen to you. As you read each "It Happened," stop at the word CHOICE? and think about what you would do if this ever happened to you before you look at the two choices I'm including.

You do not have to submit to any situation that is demeaning or dangerous to you and when you resist, there is seldom one "right" way to do it. In the following scenarios, I am only listing two options; one to submit, and one way to resist. Remember, there could be any number of ways to resist.

It Happened
You are a class officer at your school. Your duties include staying after school to help a teacher by putting up bulletin boards and grading papers. You trust and respect your teacher and have a good relationship with him. As your friendship grows, he begins telling you about personal problems he and his wife are having. **CHOICE?**

Submit: You listen sympathetically and by doing so, your emotional attachment to him becomes stronger. *BEWARE! This could eventually lead to an inappropriate, intimate relationship with this teacher.*

Resist: You remind your teacher that you respect him as your teacher but do not want to hear personal things about his life that you should not know. *This might be uncomfortable, but it will save you and your teacher a lot of grief in the long run. It is highly inappropriate for any teacher/leader to confide intimate information to his students.*

It Happened
You are lying down on the couch (facing the back of the couch) at your sister's house. Her husband lies down beside you and begins to touch your breasts. **CHOICE?**

Submit: You do not challenge his touching, because you are frightened and don't know what else to do. *BEWARE!*

This inappropriate behavior on your brother-in-law's part is bad enough on its own. However, you must realize that this is the beginning of sexual abuse which may progress to even more harmful sexual encounters with him, including rape.

Resist: You jump up, tell your brother-in-law what you think of his perversion, and demand that he never touches you again! *You might be frightened, you might not want to hurt your sister's feelings, you might be scared of how your brother-in-law will react, and you may feel unsure if the rest of your family will even believe you. Your brother-in-law will probably act like you're imagining it and play it off like it's all in your head and nothing happened. Despite all off the embarrassment and discomfort, it is worth it to react publicly to any abuse of this nature. If you don't stop this behavior right up front, you will continue to be his victim and his assaults will become more frequent and more invasive.*

It Happened

You're seventeen and at the doctor's office by yourself for the first time. As the doctor is checking your heart, he begins to press against you, breathing heavily and touching your breasts with more than his stethoscope. CHOICE?

Submit: Not knowing what else to do, you endure his "check-up."

Resist: You push the doctor away from you and tell him he is out of line. You then leave and tell your parents what happened. *Despite your discomfort and the likelihood that the doctor will deny your accusations, stand up for yourself. Do not let him get away with this assault. Your dignity and self-respect are worth protecting!*

It Happened

You are twelve years old and at your Sunday School teacher's house for a class party. He invites a couple of the girls, including you, to go see his food storage room. As you begin to walk up the stairs after seeing the room, he puts his hand up your shirt and begins to rub your back. CHOICE?

Submit: You know it's not right, but you don't know what you can do about it, so you try to ignore what he is doing. *BEWARE! Because you do not stop him from taking inappropriate liberties right up front, he then puts his hand on your leg and continues to rub it underneath the table while games are being played.*

Resist: You turn, look him in the eyes, and tell him to get his hands off you! You leave the party and tell your parents what happened. *Remember, you should never apologize for defending your dignity.*

It Happened

Your aunt and uncle are older and need help. You have been asked to go over after school and iron some shirts, as well as make up their beds. As you are making up your uncle's bed, he walks into the room, pushes you on the bed, and begins kissing you. CHOICE?

Submit: You lie there, paralyzed and confused, shocked at your uncle's behavior. *BEWARE! If you offer no resistance, your uncle has complete control over you even though he has no control over himself at that moment. This situation could very easily end with you being raped.*

Resist: You yell, hit, kick, and stage a RAGING defense. As you free yourself, you run out of the house and tell your parents what happened. *By staging your resistance any way you can, your uncle stops his assault, comes to some of his senses and leaves the room.*

It Happened

You are jogging along a trail, and as you turn a corner, you find yourself face to face with a man who is exposing his genitals to you. CHOICE?

Submit: You look shocked, embarrassed, or frightened as you cautiously move away from him. *This is what he wants. An exhibitionist gets a power rush from your discomfort.*

Resist: You could laugh and point at him. You could roll your eyes or look bored and disinterested as you continue on your way. *Showing him that you are not the least bit intimidated by his behavior will not give him the satisfaction he is looking for.*

It Happened

You are sitting in an ice cream parlor and a man approaches you, introducing himself as a modeling agent. He expresses an interest in having you model for his agency. He invites you to his home for an interview and asks you to bring your swimsuit so that he can see you in it. CHOICE?

Submit: You go to his home, swimsuit in hand for your "interview." *BEWARE! This is a common ploy sex offenders use to entice women into a secluded area (often their homes) to either photo-*

graph them while undressing or to rape them. The fact that you have been invited to his home is a pretty clear tip-off to danger.

Resist: You say, "No thank you." Now, let's pretend he did not invite you to his home, he just expressed interest and you want to check it out. Ask for a business card. Any legitimate agent and modeling agency should have business cards, an office and regular office hours. If any of these things are amiss, you should not go any further. Call the office number on the business card, drive by the address, and if you are satisfied that this agency is "for real," make an appointment and take a chaperone with you. If you feel even a touch of discomfort at any time during this process, get out immediately.

It Happened

After shopping at the mall, you find that your car has a flat tire. A seemingly nice man approaches you and offers to help you change your tire. CHOICE? You are reluctant, but he nicely insists. CHOICE? You're in a well-lit public place so you let him change your tire, and are very grateful to him for doing this dirty job. While he changes the tire, he makes conversation with you and seems to be a nice man. When he is finished, he looks at his watch and says, "Whoa, I didn't realize what time it was! I am parked clear on the other side of the mall. Could you give me a quick ride to my car so I'm not too late to an appointment?" CHOICE?

Submit: You are not comfortable letting him into your car, but because he has been so nice, you feel obligated, and you give him a ride to the other side of the mall. *BEWARE! You may never be heard from again. The man that did this had targeted his victim as she went into the mall and let the air out of her tire himself. Then he waited for her to come back out.*

118 • Be Not Afraid

Resist: There are a few places to resist in this scenario. Be very suspicious if some "nice man" just happens to appear when you have a flat tire. Learn how to change your own tires. However, there are truly nice people who will stop to help a damsel in distress. I've had a few help me before. If you are in a public place and the Spirit isn't warning you of danger, it's really up to you whether you let someone help you or not. If he helps you and then asks for a "favor" in return, there's a tip-off to danger. Remember, don't do anything for someone that you wouldn't ordinarily do, just because he seems nice, such as let him into your car and give him a ride across the parking lot. (What was he doing on this side of the parking lot in the first place?)

It Happened

You are walking down the hallway of your hotel, trying to find your room key. As you walk past a door, a man flings his door open, grabs you, and forces you into his room. **CHOICE?**

Submit: You are shocked and horrified. You feel helpless and alone, paralyzed with fear. Your attacker has complete control. *I don't think I have to tell you what could happen now.*

Resist: You suddenly find yourself in an isolated place with an assailant determined to rape and/or murder you. You begin making all the noise you can as you unleash your secret weapon and RAGE! You become the aggressor and do not stop until either you can get out of the door, someone hears the commotion and comes to help, or one of you is no longer able to attack! *Your goal is to get out of this room and you must do whatever it takes to do that.*

I hope these scenarios which other young women have been faced with have helped you visualize and practice your own personal defense skills and attitudes. If you haven't made the decision to be a resistor yet, what are you waiting for? Do it now!

In Conclusion

Can you believe I'm finally finished? I've given you everything I can think of to give you for now, and it's up to you to take it from here. It never hurts to learn more. Read more, take classes, etc. Don't ever think you know everything. I'm constantly taking self-defense classes, reading, and watching anyone who can teach me more. I realize that I might be a little more passionate about it than you'd want to be. However, please at least read and re-read this book and make your decisions about your own personal defense now. Remind yourself often of everything we've talked about and practice the tips and attitudes until they become second nature to you.

Remember, you are a daughter of God and of infinite worth to Him, to your family, to those around you, and to yourself. I know you can adopt these personal defense attitudes and once you do, you'll understand the assurance the Lord gives you as He says, ". . . Be not afraid, only believe" (Mark 5:36).

I'd like to hear from you. You can email me at:
Stacey@righteousdefense.com
if you have a story or thought you'd like to share with me
and would allow me to share with others.